YOU [illegible] CHILD'S BEST TEACHER

A Holistic Guide to Link Home and School

Revised from You Are Your Child's Best Teacher: Intentionally Linking Home and School (2012)

DeBora L'T. Mapp, EdD

Inspired Schooling Solutions
Louisville Kentucky USA

YOU ARE YOUR CHILD'S BEST TEACHER
A Holistic Guide to Link Home and School

Published by Inspired Schooling Solutions, P.O. Box 818, Louisville KY 40201

Revised from the first book: *You Are Your Child's Best Teacher: Intentionally Linking Home and School* (2012)

You are your child's best teacher: A holistic guide to link home and school. © 2015 by DeBora L'T. Mapp, EdD
ISBN-13: 978-1-5136-0077-2

Printed in the United States of America

Quantity Sales: Special discounts are available on quantity purchases by associations, initiatives and others. For details, contact the author.

Dedication

This book and series,
Speaking and Acting on the Unspoken,
is dedicated
to the peoples before us who gave so much
my beloved parents who are no longer with us,
and my seven siblings, five children, seven grandchildren
and our large and extended family and friends!

May this book be useful in giving its readers
the will, strength, courage and commitment to do what's necessary
to revitalize our families so we're ready
to think critically, feel, speak and act on the unspoken and unseen,
to meet opportunities and solve complex problems
challenging our 21st century world!

With God's help and the convergence of our wills,
we can and will get this right!

Peace!

Acknowledgements

Before writing my first book, I was challenged by a young man at a conference in New Jersey who told me that I needed to share what I knew with other people. I'd like to thank him and my sister, Angela (Angel), who told me that the four sheets of parent tips I developed for our church's back to school family ministry should be developed into a book, which became *You Are Your Child's Best Teacher: Intentionally Linking Home and School*

I was told by Msiba Ann and Chester when I presented that first 40 page book at a school and community workshop that I needed to add more of what my former husband, Jim, and I did in rearing our children. Thanks go to them for decades of support and to remind me of the decade of learning from Jimmy and Grace Boggs that changed our status quo. That required a holistic stance of this book since life and learning are layered and complex.

My daughter, Ayodele, listened to me and offered suggestions and computer advice on many aspects of that first and this revised book. Ivy, my youngest sister, and my twin sons, Obiora and Irucka, authored their first books recently and helped with this revised edition. Siku, Ava and Angela helped me immensely with the cover and final product. Memories of Mama and Daddy were with me throughout the writing.

Segun, Brenda, Toney and other family members also helped by giving me words of encouragement and critiques, suggestions to shorten my work or issues with schools they were going through. Thank you, Zariah, for your input with the student piece, and Maisha for writing your first book; and to my other grandchildren for being inspirations for my writing. Josie, thank you for the "guide." My first mentor, George the beetv, helped with my business acumen, and my new mentor Stan, Mikel and others helped to improve my book. I utilized the services of Janel, an editor, who helped me tremendously in clarifying my writing without extraneous details.

I'd like to acknowledge the many community folk and parents I met over the years as I volunteered with them and/or taught their children as we worked to make our communities in Lexington and Louisville better places to live and thrive. I learned something from all of you, even those who didn't respond, as I struggled to write a guide book that is useful for the good of all our children, our families and ultimately, our nation!

Asante sana for pushing me to finish this sojourn!

Table of Contents

Foreword

One of my mentors once commented,

We live in a world in which we are surrounded by illusions.
Illusions control you.
Once you learn to see through illusions to the essence of things, then you control the world around you.

--Dr. Frank Wallace

In "***You Are Your Child's Best Teacher: A Holistic Guide to Link Home and School,***" Dr. DeBora Mapp challenges families, schools and stakeholders to take a look at our past and present and begin reflecting on new realities. Those new realities will move us to see common denominators that reveal further connections. Those connections will enable us to strengthen our families, our schools and our country.

The 21st Century calls for new leaders to rise up and speak what those of the status quo fear to speak, "Widescope facts." Widescope facts are in actuality "Honesty" and honesty will always reveal "True Solutions."

Read this important work with an open heart and an open mind. Read it again and again, utilizing it as a reference and guide to questions you may have had in times past regarding your child's education and success. Your interest and confidence, as a parent, in your child's education WILL BE renewed! This renewal will directly affect in positive ways your local educational system and even further, our country!

YOU ARE YOUR CHILD'S BEST TEACHER!!!

Stanley D. Murphy, Ed.D.
Department Chair and
Assistant Professor
College of Arts and Sciences
Argosy University
Nashville, Tennessee

About the Author

Dr. DeBora L'T. Mapp is a speaker, author and performance consultant with Inspired Schooling Solutions which offers services to school stakeholders so they can better support learning and teaching. Dr. Mapp has had broad experiences for four decades as a teacher (P-20); district curriculum coordinator; college administrator of a first-year counseling unit; career counselor and youth director in community agencies and as a consultant. She earned an education doctorate from the University of Kentucky that emphasized educational leadership with social justice.

This book is based on Dr. Mapp's work, education, research, volunteering and home life as a granddaughter of farmers, daughter of civil rights activists with seven siblings, proud parent of one daughter and four sons and GrandMaMa to seven amazing grandchildren. These experiences helped her to understand that living, learning, teaching, schooling and our families are linked and impacted by historical, political and social forces. This requires a holistic approach to solve the many complex problems.

"My former husband and I used many of the practices in this guide while consciously making plans and decisions about our children's upbringing, rather than leaving things to chance. We successfully sought to link home learnings and community experiences with school learning.

As a public school teacher, I was reluctant even to consider private school for my children, until I visited Community Montessori School. The Montessori philosophy emphasizes freedom within limits, independence and respect for a child's natural, social, psychological and physical development. This school was a good fit for our family!

Our children flourished with a home foundation that had its problems, but we strived for wellness and well-being. We put our children on the right paths to develop plans for their futures and to become well-rounded, caring and critical thinking adults. They understand the importance of family, faith, caring for people over things, knowledge, thinking, and learning from the past, being awake and aware in the present and future hope.

Following in the footsteps of their youngest Aunt Ivy, all five of our children (one daughter and four sons) earned engineering degrees! Four of them went to graduate school and other careers and one works as an engineer. All of them followed through on earlier plans and were able to change them when later uncertainties arose, and their families are flourishing!"

Introduction

In this period of national, local and home uncertainties, adults try to make sense of changes in their lives. These changes affect their well-being through threats to employment, housing, health, education and harsher societal actions. At the same time, our children are trying to grow and develop for their places in this world as they prepare for their futures.

Children need more conscious support and love from adults during this time of uncertainties for better chances in their lives, but contradictions exist. Some of our children have had to act as mini-adults because parents didn't parent, while some adults fear some of them. They treat children harshly without teaching them how to love, learn and live peacefully.

The common thread running through this scenario is that adults and their children exist in families. Families are the basic social unit of society and they are important to society's functioning. The family unit traditionally consisted of parents, children and other relatives. Historically in our large nation, many adult children moved away from their families to faraway areas and the nuclear family of just parents and children became the norm. With more people divorced or remaining single, many families are now headed by single parents and life has become more intense in many ways.

Multigenerational families are growing in recent decades as older people live long enough to see, know and sometimes rear their grandchildren and great-grandchildren. Some adults returned to their parents' homes to live with their children, with or without jobs. In some homes, many children are not being cared for by family or neighbors so institutions, same-age friends, loneliness or technology that limits social connections help them fill their days when they are not in school.

Through all of these uncertainties, what has not changed is the responsibility of preparing children for future success: it ***still rests with caring parents*** and other adults. Parents have to make commitments to their children. Sure we're human and make mistakes at times since each child is unique, situations change, and the home environment shifts as we age and children grow and develop. But that's our job, in fact, it's the most important job in the world!

New ground is being broken in this book as we look at our families and connections to our nation's past, present and future as it takes a holistic view of life where everything is connected. Thus we have to learn from our pasts while analyzing and feeling the present to better prepare for the future. The ***goal*** of this book is to guide parents and loved ones in transforming their homes, if needed, with good parenting and relationship building skills that can help us move our families to more hope-filled futures. At the same time, we need to link what we teach children at home with learning at school since the quality of education impacts future jobs to fulfill our needs, money we earn legally and future homes to keep us safe.

The ***vision*** of this book is more satisfied and capable children prepared for learning to live in their future lives, with families ready to get them there! This is a multigenerational quest that can help you move your family to more well-being (being well-balanced, happy, prosperous and/or successful) and wellness (actively doing things to become aware of and make choices for a healthy and fulfilling life). In the process, clues in the book can help you improve the academic achievement of your children.

Clues guide you, but it takes your courage, your will to succeed and skills you build that can help you improve your family!

This book may serve as a reminder of what was done for you by your parents, what you did when you had more time and less stress, or as a guide to learn skills you didn't pick up from your home experiences. It may help you form opinions and make better decisions as you make sense of our fast-paced world as you empower yourselves for balanced families.

Because of space limitations and the need to keep from overwhelming you, some points are simplified even though we know that life is much more complicated! The guide offers evidence-based and practical advice as introductory clues to sometimes overlooked and unspoken information. These topics may remind you of what may be missing in your family. Basic and direct language with definitions will be used - most of the time.

Don't get confused with the audience of this guide book: sometimes it'll be made personal with "you," and it's written primarily for families. Yet all school stakeholders who revolve around children and their families can benefit since our roles are connected and many of us work on the same problems in our work roles and home lives. Secondarily the guide is written for student and family advocates in various initiatives to help families and children in crises and to better engage them in education.

PART I

Our Families Are Up to Us!

Success in life is founded upon attention to the small things rather than to the large things; to the everyday things nearest to us rather than to the things that are remote and uncommon.
Booker T. Washington

Families change over time. We can't go back to a better time because each time had its own problems and benefits, according to who you were and where you lived. At one point, we believed that living in certain areas kept our families insulated from what we considered were urban big city problems. But we now find these same problems occur in small rural communities and private suburban enclaves. Few are immune from problems impacting many families in our country.

We see extremes being celebrated on our many media screens seemingly without thinking about possible consequences. In addition we practice many short cuts today, like fast and microwaved foods, quick pills, reckless spending and acting without thinking. We have to stop and think about the effects of extremes and short cuts on our children's development.

What can you do to promote world peace?
Go home and love your family. *–Mother Teresa*

We have to decide if the shortcuts are compatible or incompatible with our family values, or if they will cripple our children's abilities to think about consequences as they maneuver through future uncertainties. It is more important than ever for parents and families to think about, and strengthen, their actions to prepare children for their futures. It's a life-time journey!

There are three kinds of people in the world:
those who make things happen,
those who watch things happen, and
those who wonder what happened. *–Unknown*

You are invited to come along with us on this journey – but first decide –
which kind of people are you and your family at this time?

1. The U.S. FAMILY From Past to Present

History is a story not only of the past, but of the future.
–Grace Lee Boggs, age 100

For most of recent human history, family relationships were taken for granted. We were born into a particular place at a particular time, into a set of relationships with well-defined responsibilities. We knew what to expect of others and they knew what to expect of us. When European settlers migrated to the Indians' land, they called it the New World. No matter how, why or when they arrived, immigrants, the First Peoples, Africans and Mexican Americans had to adjust. New families were created and new patterns of living were developed, without past patterns and rules. The best, worst and in between patterns were bequeathed to the future in ideals that still haven't been met.

As time passed, people made decisions to make the best of new situations and isolated conditions, always striving for the right to be free of cruelty and past inequities while sometimes inflicting it on others. They based their lives on creativity, self-reliance, reliance on others, discipline, community, commerce and initiative. Some families thrived and progressed, towns and communities grew and a new United States of America was forged, affecting peoples all over the world for good and bad.

Many contradictions exist in this land of freedom, where many have to fight for the right to life, liberty and the pursuit of happiness. Between the Civil War and World War I, newly industrialized cities grew but no people services were available. Separate but together, European American and African American women in voluntary associations developed services that grew to institutions. Since World War II we struggled and sacrificed to give our children more material things as we moved to a consumer society, losing sight of certain values important to families and our nation. Our wars fuel the economy and history lessons about them don't tell the whole story. We hold many national contradictions about freedom and how we perceive it in our country compared to ugly American stories from around the world. Perceived as the best, we treat many people the worst. We're like a maze, lost in different puzzling paths, trying to find our way.

Ideals (perfect examples) in families and our nation have shifted during the last 30 years and many more American children and families are in crisis. We placed money before people, and many families have:

- too many: emotional disruptions, divorces, material things, addictions, supersize portions and pursuits of happiness, but not of life and liberty;
- too little: money for necessities, understanding of our humanity vs. consumerism, thinking about consequences for our actions, too little time for our families and too few positive connections with others; and
- not enough: good decision making, fairness, good schools, good nutrition, wellness and well-being, working together for the common good, caring and respect for all, safety and communication; with a spiritual life that supports all the above.

Love is needed to protect our children for their futures, along with faith and hope to find solutions to problems. With love we need to offer services to others to build positive relationships through clear and creative communications.

Youth today are demanding hope, healing, love, caring relationships and solutions to overcome problems. Some of them are also demanding that they become capable of working towards the best of solutions during the worst of times. Through our efforts to link home and school, our children can be better prepared for their futures in our fast-paced, yet slow-to-change-in-some-ways, world!

We have to continually work towards balance on many levels.
Balancing family life with work, outside interests
and taking care of ourselves was needed historically.
It's still needed today and
will continue to be needed in the future
as we redefine and strengthen our families,
communities and our nation - by first starting with self.

Ordinary people can do extraordinary things.
–President Barack Obama

2. Get Started with Tough Questions

In family life, be present. --*Lao Tzu*

In our fast-paced lives today, some of us just "do" life with our families, taking little time to actually think about our actions and their possible consequences. This chapter gives you the opportunity to reflect on your family life. With our families, we have to acknowledge whether we are effective – or not – in our parenting efforts and in the choices and decisions we make in raising our children. *As you read, both parents should highlight areas of special interest.*

This is a test!

STOP ... Have you examined and evaluated what you do or don't do in and with your family? Do you make your children happy to just keep them out of your hair? Do you think about possible consequences before making tough decisions? Did you make a previous commitment to positive changes but you have not followed through yet? Are you and your family helping your children to grow and develop as you'd hoped by taking the time to learn how to do things differently?

LOOK at everything going on in your home, negative and/or positive. Do you follow the crowd even when it hurts your family's health, finances and well-being, or do you have the courage to do what's best? Do you act and look as though members of your family love each other? Do you allow your children too much freedom and not enough responsibility? Do you take time to give your children your time? Do you really see your children or just imagine what's happening with them? Is one child stuck in unhappiness? Do you reach out for help? Do you read books to your children that show pictures of children like your family?

LISTEN...hear the sounds and silences in your home. Is everybody alone on his or her favorite gadget? Is the media message negative, loud and inappropriate for your child's age? Do you cuss and fuss or smile and make peace? Do you laugh and communicate in loving ways? Do you pay more attention to your cellphone and other electronic screens than to your children?

FEEL... what your children feel as results of your actions. Are your actions positive and your home filled with light, joy, peace and love – or does your house feel sick, bullying, stress-filled and disrespectful? Are you acting as the adult? Does your home feel safe and caring? Is it comfortable? Do you practice forgiveness and gratitude?

HAVE FAITH... that your positive efforts will bring good results! It will support all you do through your beliefs that give meaning as faith guides your lives. If you need to learn more, do so. Have you noticed that when you are aware, your beliefs help in all aspects of your life?

LOVE yourself and your family enough to ***CHANGE*** or adapt how you parent and rear your children, if needed. Don't let pride stop you from reaching out for help, keep you from using tough love at times or changing your plans for more positives in your family. Choose to be courageous enough to make positive and possibly tough choices that will help prepare your children for their futures. They will grow to appreciate improvement.

GROW AND/OR CHANGE: The first steps in growth or change involve learning more about yourself so you can take control of your life -which includes your family. This requires a belief that you can do the work needed to gain new skills for success, but you have to be courageous and willing enough. No one can do this for you – you have to learn to empower yourself and your family. Today's world is more complex with technology, so try seeking the simple within the complex world we live in. Adults and children need a wide range of abilities for success today and this guide book will help you get there.

TODAY is the best time to:

- start or update the **GOOD** things in your family life;
- learn the lessons from the **PAST** and pass them on;
- be aware and awake in the **PRESENT** since it's a gift;
- do what's necessary to make the best possible **FUTURE.**

If you are ready to put this book down because you don't have the time to read, think again! Your children may appreciate the time you put into parenting and family changes. You may be pleasantly surprised at the good that can happen in your family, school and community as your home environment becomes more balanced.

3. Direct Links Exist between Home and School

We all know that parents are children's first teachers, but today's major societal changes demand that parents become their children's BEST teachers. Schools also need to become the best to prepare people's children, or their students, for society. Homes and schools share direct links for teaching our greatest resource – our children.

One was a teacher-the tools she used were books.
One was a parent with a guiding hand and a loving heart.
And each agreed she would have failed
If she had worked alone -
For behind the parent stood the school
and behind the teacher stood the home.

--Ray A. Lingenfelter

Parents should be considered as partners of schools, not clients, and schools should work to build trust with them while removing barriers. School funding and resources are more limited than they've been in a long time and the inclusion of parents as partners may be an additional helpful resource. Educators need to recognize the importance of making sure that parents are involved and engaged in the education of their children at home and school.

Parenting is the process of taking care of children and caring for them until they are old enough to take care of themselves. Parents make sure that their children are healthy and safe while preparing them to learn cultural values that then prepare them to be productive adults in society. They pass habits and goals from one generation to the next through their child rearing and parenting practices. They send their children to schools to learn more skills than they can teach them. Whether parents are good, bad or mediocre, children learn valuable lessons from them.

Teaching is the act or practice of instructing through ideas and beliefs, and schooling is the process of learning at school. Societies use education to pass habits and goals from one generation to the next. Through education and teaching, knowledge and skills are taught that affect future societal actions from schooling.

Since people don't work in isolation, relationships are needed to achieve goals like parenting and teaching. They give meaning and depth to life and are formed when we genuinely like and care for others, have something to offer them and share common goals to overcome obstacles and challenges. Clues to building relationships include: be friendly as connections are made; ask questions; tell about yourselves; go places; do things and accept others as they are. Rather than fearing rejection, assume that others want relationships with you, be persistent; get involved with others and enjoy their company. When you make mistakes in building relationships, just try something different. It takes time to sustain relationships and to keep them going so pay attention, communicate openly, appreciate each other, extend yourself, volunteer, challenge each other to do better and back each other when things get tough. [1]

In school, children become students who learn valuable lessons that can impact their lives, future families and eventually their communities and the nation. Schools should teach all students so they all achieve academically. Even when they don't, children still learn valuable lessons from them.

All students, not just the select few, should receive a good education with high standards. They all need authentic learning (dependable and relating to real life) and equity (students are taught the skills and given the experiences they need to catch up with other students) to meet each child's needs so they can learn. In the past, we used equality which is giving all children the same skills that are not matched to individual needs. With equity, teaching is not to the "middle" as usually done. Instruction is differentiated so that curriculum and instruction meet the needs of students in the same class who are smartest, average or need more support.

Many parents believe that education should transform their lives and as a result, they will have better habits and goals to pass on to their children. Many schools believe that families should better prepare their children for success in schools. What happens at school impacts the home and society and what happens at home impacts the school and society. Within a global society, it is even more important that parents and schools each do their part to prepare children, who become students in schools, for their futures.

The guidance of children is important. Parents are responsible for guiding their children from birth into adulthood with rules and beliefs. Schools, through teachers and administrators and other governmental groups, also guide students by using local, state and/or national standards and policies that carry out their beliefs through classroom curriculum and instruction.

The attitudes, beliefs and actions of both parents and schools can help or prevent students' learning. Parental attitudes about learning at home and about education and school involvement shape children's future academic achievement through your **PEACE:**

Parenting styles - are you strict, permissive, neglectful or flexible?

Expectations - do you expect a lot or a little from your children?

Aspirations - what are yours and your children's dreams and hopes?

Confidence and certainty about learning and activities that you do at home - do you believe your children can learn and you can help them do so?

Effective home rules that you expect children to follow - if not, you may not "be" there for them.

School personnel and community organizations also have attitudes and beliefs about children and learning. Their actions and beliefs can influence student learning and achievement through their **TEACH**:

Treatment of students - are students considered more favorable because of their home zip codes, English usage or skin color or are they treated fairly and represented across the school no matter their demographics?

Expectations, beliefs and assumptions about teaching and learning - do educators really believe and expect that children different from them can learn through their efforts? Do they know what to do? Do educators learn new information when needed rather than wait for staff training?

Attitudes about student and parental differences, diversity and active learning - are students and teachers actively engaged in the classroom and do teachers let their perceptions dictate limited academic growth before they really get to know your children?

Curriculum (what is taught and the hidden curriculum), how they teach (instruction), to what they evaluate (assessment), policies and discipline can dictate whether your school expects all children to learn or not.

How are available resources used for all students - are limited resources, celebrations and field trips reserved for gifted or advanced students?

Along with the community that needs to provide extra support, the shared links between **PEACE** and **TEACH** from home and school are important. Together, they should enable all children to possess the skills and capabilities to perform tasks connected to future success.

All the world awaits my coming. ...Give me a wold where I can walk talk and proud. ---- *Author Unknown*

4. Prepare for Change or Renewal

As you answered the earlier ***Tough Questions***, you may have decided that you need to change some things in your family. You may have decided that your family is doing okay, but you want to work towards renewal in a few areas. Or your organization may be using information from this guide as discussion starters and to help your clients work through different issues.

The first step towards getting somewhere is to decide that you are not going to stay where you are. -- *J. P. Morgan*

Change can lead to family renewal or the state of being made new, fresh or strong again. When you take the time to prepare for new ways of doing things, it's best that you manage your time, try to set goals and stay on an organized path to success. If you get off track, take a deep breath and get back on track. The following two strategies will help.

Keep a Journal

As you connect thinking with feeling, you'll find that writing your thoughts down comes naturally through journaling. A journal is a record of current reactions, and it's a good tool to write about your thoughts and your feelings, dreams and frustrations as you go through this guide book or your life. Keeping a journal can be relaxing and reassuring.

When you read the information later, you'll realize that you can or did work things out, or how you thought about something may have changed. It's also good for your children to keep journals so they can express their thoughts and build literacy skills. Journals, unlike diaries, do not have to be kept private, so share and discuss with the other parent and children!

Writing notes down in the Companion Journal or in your notebook while reading makes it more likely that you'll empower yourself to make changes over time. Use a different color for each child as you read about situations they're going through and the things you may need to consider doing. Record the day's date and book page numbers so you can return to that spot when needed. This works better when both parents schedule time to write as they read, then discuss the writings and reflections with each other. If it's hard to begin writing, try the following sentence starters:

1. *I need to pay special attention to…-*
2. *Actions to work on so I support my children better…*
3. *The following is tough right now…But I'm grateful for…*
4. *In school, my children are…..*
5. *I feel like I don't know what I'm doing when I… but…*
6. *Today I was glad when I saw my child…..*
7. *I'm planning on finding out more about… so I can…*

Or be creative –just write something down as you use your journal to get over your writer's block and/or parenting insecurities!

Spend time alone in objective thought as you consider the direction of your life. *--I Chin*

Plan S.M.A.R.T. F.A.M.I.L.Y. Actions

Along with journal writing as you read through this book, you may see areas that you plan to change to meet goals or results you seek. Use the following Action Plan as a guide to begin that process, knowing that there are no wrong or right ways to do it.

[After planning]…Sometimes you just need to breathe, trust, let go and see what happens. *--Mandy Hale*

An action plan is a simple list of activities and steps needed to accomplish goals or objectives. Action plans are different from to-do lists or the journal, since they focus on achieving goals and keep you from missing important steps. Since you write your plans down instead of memorizing them, it's easier to decide which activities you'll get someone else to do, or help with, or which you will work on later.

1. Decide on a Goal for your family. Goals should be ***SMART*** [2]
   Specific (clearly defined with what, why and how you'll do it);
   Measurable (use evidence so you know the goal was met);
   Achievable (it's challenging but you can achieve it);
   Results-focused (measure results, not the activities) and
   Time-bound (date or time frame you want to finish it by).

2. Identify Activities and Tasks you'll do. Start by brainstorming all needed actions and write them down in case you don't need them all for this first time. Work on one or two areas at a time. Determine the first step and what should happen next. Is it logical or do you need to go back to an earlier step to rearrange your activities and tasks? Are there any deadlines to be aware of? Any costs?

3. Delegate Tasks and Analyze Your Steps – after you write the goal you are meeting, write the steps of the project from beginning to end, double-checking each action. Decide which family member will take responsibility for which task and consult their schedules. If there are any barriers, note how you will work around them. How much time will it take? How will you know the goal is met?

4. Final Check to Finish: make sure your plan is complete by using the FAMILY mnemonic (letters representing words) as clues:

    Funds or money needed, if any;
    Actions/activities or tasks; area or space needed;
    Materials and resources to help you meet goals;
    Individuals or tools needed;
    Leadership or person responsible for each step;
    Your family can celebrate after as goals are met!

While working on the Action Plan, keep it with you. Learn from the Action Plan by revising it or noting in your journal what you could have done better, after family discussions. This is a good tool for many family and work projects. Your child can also use this process to plan actions for assigned major projects and individual success!

We can begin by doing small things at the local level, like planting community gardens or looking out for our neighbors. That is how change takes place in living systems, not from above but from within, from many local actions occurring simultaneously. --*Grace Lee Boggs*

All of us know that parents are their children's first teachers, and you would/should/could be your children's BEST teachers, ready and willing to take the time to transform yourselves while linking home with school on the journey to successful futures!

Do not only think about it, but feel about it also, before taking appropriate action. – T.F. *Hodge*

5. Direct Links Also Exist between Thinking and Feeling

The value of an education…is not the learning of many facts but the training of the mind to think. *–Albert Einstein*

Thinking and feeling are a part of living. Today we hear a lot about how children and adults feel in media and our day to day lives. When we spend a lot of time either feeling or thinking, we can sometimes leave out the sensing, knowing and being that connect them. Direct links exist between thinking (action of using the mind to produce thought) and feeling (awareness of an emotional state or reaction). We may believe that feelings and emotions are caused by external forces like the words or actions of others. But our thoughts and beliefs happen quickly and automatically, determining or influencing how we perceive or feel.

As our babies grow physically, they develop emotionally and they experience different feelings like anger, fear, sadness and happiness. They develop higher order feelings like shame and embarrassment by age two and guilt, envy and pride by age three. They don't know what their emotions mean and they don't have the vocabulary to express how they feel so they bite, hit, shout or cry. They may later develop temper tantrums when things are out of balance and not right with them. By the time your toddlers grow to school age, they learn to express their feelings a little better with words.

With pre-adolescents, we easily see physical changes at puberty as their bodies mature. They also experience cognitive (thinking) and social and emotional changes in how they react to others and in their own personalities. Normal feelings and behaviors from middle to high school can be grouped into major areas of moving toward future interests and independence, cognitive development and sexuality, ethics (morals) and self-direction.

Teenager was a new term in the early 1940s and adolescence came a few decades later with middle school reform. Other new phenomena during this last shift in forces included helicopter parents who hover over their children and solve too many of their problems; children who stay in late adolescence until their 30s; and grandparents and great grandparents who may raise their children's children or great-grandchildren.

Each of these groups sometimes deal with feelings as more important than thinking at times and sometimes consequences for behaviors may not be thought about. Many of them focus on superficial thinking and how they look. Media caters to them with reality shows and gaming that looks at the worst and most extreme of human behaviors. Fortunately, researchers speculate that when children are expected to grow up, they do, and many families are functioning as they should. They are able to separate thinking from feeling and carry on their lives in the same fast-paced world, though sometimes with different results.

Whether you think you can or you can't, you're right. --*Henry Ford*

Along with thinking, feeling is important when coupled with common sense or intuition. Gut reactions and feelings are intuition, but they can be based on mood and other psychological factors. Look at your feelings to see if your emotions and beliefs are getting in the way of common sense and thinking at times. Relying mostly on feelings and emotions can cause more trouble in life, no matter what stage you're in.

For common sense, you have to be able to reflect on your thinking by looking at the bigger picture while taking time to work through your thoughts and feelings. When we know how to do things while being open minded and curious, it helps us link feelings with thoughts more easily. When common sense and learning what to do are linked with thinking and positive feelings, good things can happen.

Thinking and feeling in school. Public schools prepared Americans to be good citizens and good factory workers for more than a century. Students were required to sit still, listen and do exactly as they were told. This type of thinking was simple, transparent, sure and repetitive until it became a habit. Students who followed this way of thinking were considered obedient when they followed the rules.

The above is an example of lower-order thinking. These skills support basic skills in reading and writing and they are easier to understand, teach, test and learn, so many schools and parents still use them. We'll always need lower-order thinking skills, but we need to learn other thinking skills to be proficient or skillful in dealing with recent changes.

Today's adults and students need higher-order thinking and feeling skills:

- be curious (so ask questions) and be able to think quickly;
- understand decision making with links to consequences;

- know how to set priorities (determine what's most important);
- strategize (plan and manage);
- feel comfortable with identifying issues that need to be solved with opportunities to improve the system and relationships;
- collaborate (work together peacefully in groups) with others.

Higher-order thinking requires more interactions and some consider it messier than lower-order thinking. Within their peer groups, many children use some of these skills on a daily basis. But schools and some families following old school rules still keep the lower-order thinking skills as most important to how they function and what they expect.

Think critically. In addition to higher-order thinking skills, adults and students need critical thinking skills. [3] Critical is defined as relating or being at a major turning point. Critical thinking is the ability to think clearly (not confused, using reasons without bias, prejudice, hopes and fears) and rationally (logically without impulse). This thinking is complex (not simple) and requires creative thinking (out of the box or different) and problem solving, questioning, effort and possibly many solutions.

Critical thinking is not a natural skill. Some critical thinking decisions are complex and solutions may not seem obvious, so multiple strategies or clues have to be used or applied to solve problems. Critical thinking is shaped by beliefs and processing skills that are used to manage and modify (or change) actions as you investigate options and reach conclusions.

Process skills involve observing, putting into order, communicating, measuring, guessing and predicting. These are skills you introduce at home. In order to process and think, people need to be open-minded, develop curiosity, plan and strategize, be careful and think critically. Then they need to think again, making sure to feel where they are in the process! People use these skills many times a day so just relax and know that you and your children can be successful in thinking and feeling.

Inform your children about the importance of being proactive, or acting before something happens, and to think about possible consequences for their actions. Wherever we are, proactive thinking can be the thin line between life and death. Parents need to get used to talking about some of their thoughts and feelings at home so children get used to doing this.

Critical thinking takes work and it's not simple. It's hard to find examples of different thinking strategies in one place. Thus, a few clues to think critically are offered here. They will help you better link home with schooling as your family moves to more proficiency with adult life and children's academic achievement.

Ask Questions before Making Decisions

1. Use the 6 W's: who, what, where, when, why and how.
2. Examine supposed facts: is there supporting evidence?
3. Are arguments just emotions or are they real reasons?
4. Is there more than one good answer or explanation?
5. Did past events possibly impact decisions you make now? Note that what you see and feel now may be based in your past, not the present.
6. Do you think about what you already know or can learn to create new ideas and information that may raise even more questions?
7. For higher-order thinking, can you:
   a. Visualize the problem?
   b. Separate relevant information from irrelevant?
   c. Seek reasons and causes? Justify solutions?
   d. See more than one side of a problem?
   e. Decide which resources are credible and /true?
   f. Talk about un-real assumptions rather than real reasons?
   g. Identify bias or logical inconsistencies?
8. Are you aware that in everyday conversations or in media ads, propaganda may be used to make arguments more persuasive? Used on purpose or by mistake, these methods are not based on facts:
   a. Name calling (tear the opponent down);
   b. Get on the bandwagon (everybody's doing it);
   c. Glittering generalities (use important-sounding, empty words);
   d. Testimonial (use a celebrity to endorse a product);
   e. Card stacking (put a lot of things in your favor);
   f. Either/or fallacy (when something may be in-between);
   g. Faulty cause & effect (one thing did not necessarily cause it);
   h. Appeal to ignorance (if no one proved false, it must be true);
   i. Straw man (exaggerate or simplify so it seems ridiculous).
9. Write a list of pros and cons for any situation. Does one outweigh the other? Still can't decide? Talk to others or do research online to see how others handled the problem, making sure you look at the author of the information (if it's someone's opinion, it may not be best source).
10. Make sure that you use common sense with feeling and thinking!

Wisdom is not the product of schooling
but the lifelong attempt to acquire it. --*Albert Einstein*

6. Dressed to Impress…

What we need at the most fundamental level
is a shift in worldview, grounded in a willingness
to see more and exclude less.
Instead, too many of us live in willful denial. --*Tony Schwartz*

I asked some questions in the earlier *Tough Questions* chapter and made some statements that may have made you feel that I was meddling in your business. They were meant to shake you a little bit, to wake you for reactions so that you really feel what's going on in your home, not just casually think about it.

We are going through some perplexing times right now. Sometimes you may feel you need to shake your head to make sense of what you hear and see on media programming, on line or even hear in some conversations! Our children and our family's futures are intertwined with national uncertainties in real time because of technology.

We live amid contradictions where truth and falsities occur at the same time with misconceptions or wrong information about many things. These contradictions and misconceptions are puzzling and have been prevalent throughout our history and within many day to day occurrences. Some of our families are so caught up in them, they seem to have lost their way!

This reminds me of the story about the ruler who wanted to dress to impress. He was promised an outfit that was invisible to people considered unfit for their positions, unwise or incompetent. In order not to be seen that way, nobody dared say they didn't see the new outfit. It took a child to shout the obvious - out of the mouths of babes!

Our country has ***dressed to impress*** since before our founding in 1776. Bits of our history seem larger than life since our revolutionary ideas were changing the world. Ordinary people were talking about the high ideals of self-governance, rather than be subjects of kings and emperors of the feudal system. Our nation began right before the industrial revolution when capitalism was considered as a progressive economic system when compared to feudalism. The size of this country gave unlimited opportunities when you didn't factor in the people already living here who believed that the land belonged collectively to the People. Our country continues the tradition of dressing to impress.

Future generations were ***promised an outfit but it's invisible to the people.*** Life, liberty and the pursuit of happiness were promised to U.S. citizens, but our government did not develop so that it would be responsible for the good of our society in areas benefitting all the people as they worked to reach those ideals. The outfit that's invisible could be freedom, according to how it's defined.

If our forefathers and foremothers had done things differently, socially and politically responsible decisions would have been normal in our society. The ideals of balancing power with justice, equality, courage and honesty would have forced us to make different decisions for centuries. Well-meaning activists have always had to fight our local, state and national governments for amendments and laws to benefit the people and our Earth for needs like clean air and water, safe housing, jobs, fairness, etc.

People considered unfit, unwise, incompetent - or different. This can be likened to how we treat some people in our country today. The U.S. has always had diversity or the inclusion of different people within our country. Historically we have been the most internationally and religiously diverse country in the world and we still are today. Many interpret differences in our population as bad or inferior, not just as facts. At its most basic level, diversity is variety or difference.

Diversity, unity and inclusion could/would/should work together!

With diversity comes the handling or mishandling of relationships. Relationships are the ways that two or more people talk to, behave toward and deal with each other. Relationships are supposedly important to our functioning as a nation developed "for, of and by the people" as we unified states into one nation. Some of us never get the relationship part right because of our contradictions and misconceptions.

Relationship problems started early in our nation's history and many Americans live in denial about how they were and are handled on many levels. Some national and educational decisions contradictory to our ideals were made throughout our history and sometimes in our families to the present day. Contradictions allow some of us to stay blinded to the use of power, control and privilege that favor one group over others. Power is control over others, and privilege is assumed rights or benefits over others. Our many "isms" like sexism, classism, racism, individualism, etc. seem normal since we try to pretty up many of our discriminatory attitudes.

Out of the mouths of babes. Our children are trying to inform us about our lives today that border on this story, but many of us are not listening. All across the country some of our youth are raising their voices as they search for purpose in their lives. Fortunately, some protest inequities in our society, serve others and try to be their best selves. While a few try to join the wrong side in foreign wars, join hate groups or gangs, some choose to inflict hurt on themselves and others. We have a lot of work to do to save our children, but we need to save ourselves, too!

Some of us haven't taught our children the history of our families nor our country. Their knowledge includes many gaps in how and why we live a certain way; how and why we need to get along with others different from our family; and why and how we need to do more than just survive, but need to thrive. Some of us adults don't even know the how's and why's! We need to do better for our children so they can do better for their children and families, including the bigger systems of our community, city, state and our country. We are not in this alone!

To cope with a changing world,
any entity must develop the capacity of shifting & changing–
of developing new skills and attitudes;
in short, the capability of learning. -- A De Gues

History and education can help us to better understand our personal selves, our collective lives and some of our contradictions as Americans. Some of us have to read between the lines while thinking critically to cause a shift in how we see the world. What we learn can help us build better relationships but it depends on how we learn.

We need to know who benefits from certain information about others. We need to struggle to overcome personal bias and prejudged opinions since they make us feel threatened while we may threaten others. Most importantly, we need to guard against refusing to believe something just because we wish some contradictions to remain true or false. Some of us even refuse to get to know other cultures because of this.

As we see more, we can then use what we've learned from formal and informal education and history to become more responsible and more engaged peoples capable of solving complex issues that are problems in our complex world today. We exclude less when we work on building relationships with others, beginning with ourselves. Then we can move to doing our best. Some of us are where we need to be at this time, but some of us are still hurting from past and recent events.

Healing from the past is necessary. We can then consider more positive changes within our families and our country as we become proficient and more skillful in working with recent changes. In order to move from where we are to more family success, some people may need to fill in historical blanks with more of the whole story to understand their people, and possibly find out more about their family. Learn more if needed, so you can choose to break old habits and patterns possibly based in negative parts of your past.

The aftermath of nonviolence is the creation of the beloved community, while the aftermath of violence is tragic bitterness…. [A]nother element that must be present in our struggle that …makes our resistance and nonviolence truly meaningful… is reconciliation. Our ultimate end must be the creation of the beloved community. --*Dr. Martin L. King Jr.*

7. … with Nowhere to Go

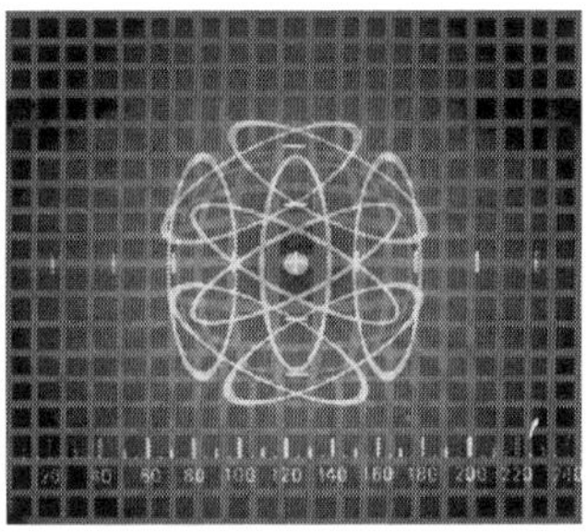

To move towards the beloved community, we have to do things differently. We have to acknowledge that our actions do not occur in isolation since what we do in one area affects other areas. To gain solutions to complex challenges today, we have to shift our basic assumptions and understandings of relationships, connections, prediction and control, since they are constantly changing qualities. This requires faith since we can't see connections concretely but we need to know they exist.

We can guess, but can't predict or control even our children's future lives since they have agency as human beings, or the right to make their own choices. We can offer our children clues, but they use them as they choose. We try to raise them right so hopefully they'll make the best decisions from their choices. During this crucial period that's pivotal to our future as a country, many more of us need to choose to make changes for the good of our families, our communities and our nation.

Some of the previous contradictions may cause you to question what's going on, or you may think about those things briefly and find they don't fit how your particular family lives. They're somebody else's problems we figure. You may have thought some of the problems about privilege, power and diversity were dealt with when we elected our nation's first African American President, or that the issues had been laid to rest or solved because hundreds of years passed. Centuries have passed and some of us continue to be baffled. Some things that bother us are unspoken topics that we encounter, like family secrets or the hidden curriculum at school. They're there but polite people don't bring them up. They're secrets even though in-your-face problems sometimes occur as results of past actions around them! We have to learn to face them and our history!

We are not held accountable for what happened before we were born, but we need to do better as we know better.

We have a lot on our national and family plates. Our nation is losing ground when compared to other advanced industrialized countries. Among them, we have the highest high school drop-out rate in the world; we are number one in children living in poverty and we have more jailed people than any other country in the world! We also have problems with increasing health concerns and how we treat our children. Our children need fairer chances and we need to stop placing them at risk for failure in school and in life. We are definitely not dressed to impress!

We move from one crisis to another, not learning lessons from our history to find solutions. We hope that the last crisis and decreasing economic problems in our country will trickle down to our families again with high standards of living and social reforms, along with school reforms that work this time. Where will we go with the following issues that need solutions?

1. Many of us search for well-being and wellness in bottles of liquor or drugs, sex or extreme behaviors rather than changing how we live so we develop ourselves to feel hopeful and work for a better world.
2. Our foods, bodies, health and planet are compromised by legal chemical innovations. They impact obesity, climate change, unclean air, toxins exposures and too many food allergens with too much emphasis on disease and not enough on prevention and wellness.
3. Our culture pits the haves and the have-nots against each other, and some families are uncertain which group they belong to or should support since more than income determines the haves.
4. Some call for "good" Americans to carry weapons for protection, and build jails for "others" not in their group.
5. Our justice system jails more Black young adults than 50 years ago.

6. Some parents are afraid of the children they raised, so refuse to discipline them; some laws prefer no hitting but they offer no alternatives while a few law enforcers kill with no mercy.
7. Injustices and unfair zero tolerance policies are allowed in education: some kindergarteners with temper tantrums are handcuffed; the school to prison pipeline is started with 3rd grade reading difficulties; too many students are unfairly pushed out of school with suspensions and expulsions which lead to future drop outs; parents are arrested for seeking better schools for their children and private privileged programs sometimes occur within troubled public schools.
8. Some of us are shaken in our faith and spirituality with the lack of trust in some of our ministers who are unethical and unprincipled. Benjamin Franklin wrote about this centuries ago!
9. Too many of us see, hear and speak no evil, though we support it by participating (our favorite actors do it!) and being avid viewers and story tellers of its effects. Is it right or wrong? Do we really care?
10. Our children rank extremely low in social and emotional well-being. Poverty, race and social class are said to explain some of this, but it cuts across these areas. Largely ignored is the responsibility of all of us to change society so it benefits all of our children and adults, too!
11. Too many children are committing suicide, and some of them seem to be taking the brunt of misplaced hate. Too many families are killing their children and our children kill or hurt themselves and each other. Violence needs to be replaced with "beloved community" attributes.
12. Some of our children don't like to read so some skills can be lost over the years. Some jobs will be lost when future employers look at social media postings that show too much skin and too many negatives.
13. Too many people seem unable to cope with life's ordinary demands and routines, possibly with the beginnings of mental illnesses that could start with minor physical, psychological or emotional problems. Too many children are placed in harm's way and need to be kept safe.
14. We use quick fixes for short periods of time when long term commitments by education, government and business are needed to reduce problems that impact family well-being and wellness.

We do not have a money problem in America.
We have a values and priorities problem. *–Marian Wright Edelman*

Many of the above 14 points are issues related to relationships. Today so much is going on in our country. We have many innovations and new gadgets that keep some of us from paying attention to disconnects and breakdowns in our society and families. At the same time our nation seems to be going backwards to "olden" days that limited and excluded. Some consider it to be a better time in our nation because people were kept in their place. The times were not good enough then for everybody and are definitely not good enough now.

Are we learning lessons from the past for a better future and our collective right to life, liberty and the pursuit of happiness for all the people? We can't leave these issues to politicians from any of the parties since they all seem the same when it comes to people issues in our country.

Nowhere to go. A major misconception and unspoken issue at the heart of what we do is consumerism. Consumerism is the theory that an increasing consumption or use of goods is economically desirable in our capitalist economic system. We have to buy since it helps our economy. We never talk about it, but just buy it! It may be in the back of our minds that we buy too much of the latest and most expensive when the old is still good, but we figure that everybody else is doing it, so we do, too!

Too many families have low incomes and more with middle incomes are joining them. Our buying mentality leaves many us with nowhere to go. We can't continue with our heads in the sand about relationships and trying to buy happiness. From producers in the past, we have become a nation of consumers who deplete natural resources while generating waste.

Some of us make decisions heavily influenced by the unknown "Joneses" and aggressive business marketing. Many of us put our blinders on as we spend with credit cards, coupons, rewards and discount stores on every corner for spending more while earning less. Each American generation has done better than the one before them and what we do impacts the next generation. But something different is happening in the 2010s.

Nationally, our children in this generation will not earn more money than their parents' generation for the first time since the founding of our nation. A contradiction with this is that we have gotten them used to a lot of things that cost a lot of money. Some of us, and our children, have become addicted to electronics and we don't pay enough attention to our children. Some of us haven't taught our children moderation in all things so they feel that being on the edge of extreme is good for them. The contradiction in consumerism is that human needs have to be met since

people are more than just consumers. [4]

We have physiological or bodily needs for nutritious foods, shelter, clothing and clean air and water, security and protection. People also need relationships for love and a sense of belonging, recognition, status and a sense of self. Belief in a positive sense of self includes: self-efficacy (being capable), self-confidence (personal worth), self-discipline (will power), self-respect (value self), self-concept (beliefs about self), self-image (mental picture of your body) and self-love (trust that you can love yourself and others can love you, too).

When people don't believe in themselves, they are more apt to focus on pleasure and selfish desires being met so they feel in control of something. This is done even at the expense of some families' needs and well-being. Spending money on the latest advertised whatever, over-stimulating our senses and emotional eating can become a way of life. They help us feel better for a while until our health suffers and we have to rob Peter to pay Paul again. Some of us feel the pressure and stress in our lives as we value things more than faith. We may not consciously think about how our choices and decisions impact our health and our children's present and future lives. Some of us sometimes act as if we don't know what's right and what's wrong because of the decisions we repeatedly make.

It's good that many of us are still into doing the best that we can through our spiritual practices, helping ourselves improve and reaching out to help others. Many of us gain satisfaction from working and producing, and we're still interested in working on human possibilities with its ideals of fairness, freedom, participation, social relations and living in harmony with nature that are so needed.

You can undermine or support your family's well-being with your lifestyle choices and your children learn these skills from you, their parents. Do you want your lifestyle to continue as it is, or do you see areas needing change? Hopefully you had time to think, feel and now know that balance is needed in your family's life. We have to deal with ourselves so more of us can move on to better ways of living!

People are aware that they cannot continue in the same old way but are immobilized because they cannot imagine an alternative. We need a vision that recognizes that we are at one of the great turning points in human history when the survival of our planet and the restoration of our humanity require a great sea change in our ecological, economic, political, and spiritual values.

--*Grace Lee Boggs* [5]

PART II

The Continuing Saga of Living and Learning

Live as if you were to die tomorrow.
Learn as if you were to live forever. *–Mahatma Gandhi*

A saga is a long detailed account of stories, and as long as families live and learn, they continue to add to the detailed stories of their lives. Schooling plays a big part in that accounting since societies and schools are intertwined. Schools and families need to continually change to keep up with the times to improve their functions. Schools call their changes reforms, while families empower themselves to renew or improve.

Education reform has changed some aspects of schooling over the years, but few of them were meant to make sure that all children learn. We continue our grade to grade system from the days of the Model T Ford car with its step-by step progression. The automobile industry had to evolve to keep pace with society, individual choice and the environment. As competition with foreign countries grew, that industry had to change to continue to make returns on its investments.

Education tries to evolve to keep pace but it is an unwieldy system funded at the whim of politicians and controlled by the sometimes limited training and beliefs of some school stakeholders. Many people remember how they were educated, and they don't want changes for their children – even though the world has changed and many of their children aren't prepared. We allow computers, sure, but the methods, curriculum and instruction as taught in some colleges of education have not kept pace with the times and they have not taught many of today's teachers what's best for all students.

Learning is not a product with profits, but if we invested in all our children our nation could wield big benefits. A major issue that we try to control in education is that of how we treat diverse students and adults, which is a relationship problem. We allow a few students not in the majority to enjoy the benefits of the best education, but that will probably change as the minority becomes the majority in some schools. Reform at this stage is like putting a bandage on a finger when the arm is broken.

We have known for a while that teacher performance is key to student learning. The performances of all school stakeholders have to evolve and change so they can better support the interactions of teachers and students in classrooms so "Every Child Achieves." They can if we have the will, courage, skills, dispositions or right attitudes and knowledge to do so.

Lives [and schools] fall apart when the foundation upon which they were built needs to be re-laid.
Lives [and schools] fall apart, not because God is punishing us for what we have or have not done.
Lives [and schools] fall apart because they need to... they weren't built the right way in the first place. --*Iyanla Vanzant*

During this period of rapid change, you may have lost your job or your home. You might have gotten sick or been injured. To get through these challenging experiences that may have rocked your world, you had to continually learn how to perform better by doing something different – you had to change. Hopefully you became capable of dealing with life's challenges by becoming more proficient, or skilled, in learning how to right things that were wrong. You also became literate or educated in knowing how to deal with those issues.

Proficiency is the knowledge and experiences needed for success. It's not the highest level of learning, but it means you have the skills to be successful. You want your children to be proficient in learning the skills they need to be successful in school and life. As a normal part of raising children, parents introduce skills and experiences so children can become capable or able to do things and literate or educated as they learn at home.

Literacy is a collection of shared cultural and communication practices that change with society and technology. People have always had to adjust to what was happening in their communities around literacy, but today being literate requires a shift in thinking from the simple and clear cut literacy of the past. Being literate used to mean knowledge of the

3 R's of ***R***eading, w***R***iting and a***R***ithmetic.

The need for proficiency in literacy and other skills and attitudes are more important now with rapid societal and technological changes.

You probably already introduce some of the following points to your children in preparation for becoming more **LITERATE** for living in today's global society. If not, teach your children while you learn more, if needed, about your community and other parts of the world with them.

Learn continually throughout your life while using innovative strategies;
Interest your family in being active in communities to improve them;
Think critically to make good decisions to gain better solutions to issues;
Evaluate situations before acting, look for connections and be flexible;
Remember to build positive relationships and link family values to them;
Apply what's learned at home to school, life, careers and job training;
Take time to learn innovation skills to be capable, creative and literate;
Engage and share in cultural literacy experiences and yours and others' cultural identities to better communicate across cultures.

All of our students should possess adequate understandings of many things, which is proficiency in a nutshell.

- In school they need to have satisfactory knowledge or enough knowledge to understand standards and course content.
- They need to demonstrate they can understand challenging subjects and skills, and apply or use them in real-world situations.
- They apply or use skills that analyze (by studying) and investigate (by observing and examining). Students answer and ask questions that are matched with school and life situations.

Proficient performance levels are adequate understandings of school standards. Performances are actions or things that people do. Standards are models or examples chosen by those in authority for teachers to teach students. Proficiency is level 3 in a 4 level system.

- Level #4: thorough understandings of standards and content that students apply or use as they solve problems.
- Level #3: proficient or adequate understandings of some standards and content applied to solve problems.
- Level #2: partial understandings with limited or few applications used in solving problems.
- Level #1: minimal or the least understandings for what needs to be done to solve problems.

The downside of using performance levels is its use with many tests or assessments so educators can possibly determine if students are learning from year to year. All students, not just some, have to show academic growth every year and are expected to learn at proficient levels so they can figure out our world to become more successful in their future lives. Being smart at school begins at home with parents as the best teachers.

8. Achievement: One of Many Education Gaps

Many Americans have faith in the power of education to transform society, and some want it to ultimately help them transform their family lives. Education, both formal and informal, can help people overcome some of life's obstacles. The U.S. has never had quality education for all and social and economic inequities have always been intentionally reproduced in our school systems to mirror society. The past is over, but it passed down to our 21st century (2000s) generation some problems from the 17th (1600s) century around relationships and how we treat people.

It was clear to me as a civil rights leader in the '60s that unless we put the social and economic underpinnings beneath political and civil rights, we wouldn't go anywhere.

-- Marian Wright Edelman

These differences produce gaps as obstacles or circumstances that keep people apart and prevent progress. Many have learned how to make-do with substitutions at times, but the lack of a good education has few substitutes. The gap of not learning enough can have far reaching consequences on fulfilling family needs and wants and on our country.

An important fact about a major inequity in our nation. Few rural (not in cities) southerners of either race went beyond the 8th grade until after **1945**. Just nine years later (**1954**), racially segregated schools were declared inferior to other schools by the Supreme Court. We may wonder why "they" don't seem as smart as others who had more learning advantages.

Education reform continued with a few strategies to keep peace in schools that reluctantly accepted students of color and consolidated rural schools. Few schools and educators were prepared for the new changes since structural (the organization of schools) and relationship problems in our country were still being reproduced in our educational system. Some changes were positive, like cooperative learning and multicultural education, but some of them were not. Some children were seen by many as intellectually, and sometimes other ways, inferior, for various reasons.

Schooling progress had been reported for years in national reports, but disparities or differences between student groups were overlooked. They were overlooked until 1986 when the National Alliance of Black School

Educators developed a way to look at data to determine gaps in academic achievement among different demographic groups. This new process was called disaggregation as it separated students from diverse demographic groups located in the census, like race, family income, gender, etc.

The education achievement gap is the difference in achievement between students from diverse groups compared with European American students. No longer could differences be overlooked since data told who was achieving and who was not! All students were and are not presently achieving academically. Around **2000**, the federal government finally held public schools accountable for the academic achievement of all students. Some school districts have been working for more than twenty years to close gaps in achievement and they are still working at it.

During the **2010**s, another major population shift occurred with more growth in the Hispanic/Latino/a population and a decline in European Americans. With that and a steady rise in the number of Asian American and multi-racial students with flat growth of African American students, the former minority has outgrown the majority in some schools. Plus, test scores of some Hispanic and Latino students rose above some African American students in some schools. We have a lot of work to accomplish to prepare all students for more successful futures by engaging and teaching them or the gaps will continue to grow.

Education gaps also appear in grades, test scores, course selections, dropout rates, college completion rates, suspension rates, course offerings, grade retention rates, attendance in dropout factory schools, lower math and reading achievement, behavioral problems and risk of interpersonal and self-directed violence. These gaps appear in a mix of factors across race, income and family structures, English language proficiency (how well students speak English) and learning disabilities.

These gaps persist even when children are in the same class, supposedly receiving the same information. So, something else is happening in our classrooms! Differences in achievement levels occur because of complex reasons. Could relationship issues be part of the problem since most schools do little to acknowledge bias and prejudged opinions that disregard equity and fairness in how we treat some diverse students?

Some students of all races and incomes have always achieved excellence, got good jobs and became leaders due to their home lives, in spite of their formal schooling. Those who were privileged usually had the best teachers, schools and resources. Many students not in the privileged group were not achieving as well, but that was expected and considered normal. It helped support the US economy by providing a steady stream of industrial and service labor.

It's like one thing influences the other, historically and today as education has been used to control housing and jobs. When people are not educated, they can't get better jobs nor better housing, and the tax base for their segregated and unequal schools is based on their housing and incomes. This was no accident but done to keep people, who used to be considered as property or from the wrong side of the tracks, in their places. On different levels, government developed laws to support these practices for centuries. The haves and the have-nots have long been a part of U.S. life!

When schools were desegregated or opened to previous students not allowed in some cities, access to housing and jobs away from segregated areas increased but with the loss of small businesses over decades. As people lost jobs, parent and child homelessness grew. As usual, contradictions still existed. Housing laws still function today in some areas to keep certain people out of some neighborhoods, schools and some out of jobs. Frustrated segregated communities with limited job opportunities, schools that don't teach skills needed to move ahead and inadequate services may influence some recent uprisings in our cities.

Gaps during the last 20 years also grew in skills and behaviors related to civic engagement and a lack of social trust among students overall. These behaviors include less participation by lower income and some middle income students in volunteering, academic clubs, community participation, extracurricular activities and sports. Self-imposed screen time isolation may keep some students away from positive participation in these areas.

Public schooling has gone through many changes as schools reformed, bringing to the forefront more contradictions and misperceptions. Jobs and higher education are recent goals, but too many of our children are still homeless and hungry because their parents don't make enough money or don't have jobs. We play at doing democracy which is simply defined as government by the people with rules of the majority winning. But we don't talk much about how to live it, achieve it, sustain it or how to keep it going when we do have it.

Democracy needs to be re-born in each generation and education is its mid-wife. – *John Dewey*

Gaps can be closed if we have the will, commitment & courage!!

9. National Standards to the Rescue!?

The reality of living in our society includes contradictions which have already been mentioned. They show up as disparities or inequalities that effect the types of jobs we can get, our access to good education, housing, medical care and even nutritious foods. These inequalities have undermined public education goals and possibly your family goals for generations, from the amount of money you earn to the expansion of your civil rights. Civil rights are the nonpolitical rights of citizens as guarantees of personal liberty by the U.S. Constitution. Schooling is a civil right.

It is impossible to struggle for civil rights,
equal rights for Blacks, without including Whites.
Because equal rights, fair play and justice are all like the air:
we all have it, or none of us has it. ... *--Maya Angelou*

Each state has worked on reforming education for decades. The federal government had to finally lead the way because of many different issues related to unfairness, inequities and other problems. As we left the 20th century and stumbled into the 21st century, national groups with the government finally worked together to set national standards for education.

Following is more technical information, but it could be the reason as to why you bought this particular guide along with Part III!

The national standards are known as ***Common Core State Standards*** (CCSS). They are meant to prepare all graduating students for their futures, no matter where students live, how much money their parents make, their race nor ethnicity. The standards are considered as practical and realistic. They are being challenged by groups who have their own perspectives about them. They are closer than anything else we've done to make sure that all U.S. students are educated so they have the skills to take advantage of future opportunities, though the standards do have some problems.

Information on the common core is paraphrased (written in my own words) from the CCSS website. [6] CCS standards are a state led effort to give all students the skills and knowledge needed for yearly progress and after-graduation success. They should help students prepare for entry-level careers, training or higher education after graduation and for success in life. They were designed collaboratively by state governors, heads of education and educators. For the CCSS, the best standards already used by states were aligned or matched with expectations from colleges, workforce training programs, employers and expectations from other countries.

The standards are also "research and evidence based; clear, understandable and consistent; aligned with college and career expectations; based on rigorous content and application of knowledge through higher-order thinking skills" (CCSS, 2010). The standards are engaging so they should interest students. They are aligned with deeper learning by using higher order thinking skills so students have the knowledge to understand societal goals and how to live more successfully within society.

In an earlier chapter, thinking skills were explained and shown to be important for all students and adults. When you read the original CCSS you will notice that it uses lower-order thinking skills, such as knowledge, comprehension and application, which is lower and higher order thinking.

To learn deeply, students need to use higher-order thinking skills that show connections across many subjects. They include application (using what is available), analysis (break into parts and examine them), logic (thinking in rational ways), evaluation (determine worth), critiques (consider benefits), inference (guess), connections (joined), synthesis (combining parts), reflection (think about) and metacognition (thinking about thinking).

You can learn more about the Common Core State Standards in different formats as mentioned earlier. You can find your state's standards at standards-in-your state, report cards for your state, [7] school [8] and the *PTA Parents' Guides to Student Success.* [9] Some states are still reforming their standards since they now have to show more effort so "Every Child Achieves" [10] and shows academic growth each year.

Emphasized Subjects Designed with the most advanced current thinking in the U.S. and internationally benchmarked, the Common Core State Standards should prepare students for success in college or training after high school, in careers and in life. Common Core State Standards emphasize and focus on two major subject areas. They are the two subjects that are used to build skill sets in other subject areas:

1. ***English/Language Arts (ELA) and Literacy in History, Social Studies, Science and Technical Subjects***
2. ***Mathematics***

CCS standards help students prepare for success after graduation. The standards use clear and consistent guidelines for what students should know and be able to do at each grade level in English Language Arts and Mathematics. Students are not limited to learning only grade-level standards each year, but they can move ahead as they reach proficiency.

- In kindergarten to eighth grade, grade by grade standards are integrated or taught together in various subjects.
- In grades 9-12, standards are grouped into two year bands (9th-10th and 11th-12th) that supplement or support subjects.

The standards allow teachers to measure student progress. They also help ensure that students are on the path to academic achievement and life success with the goal of college and entry-level career readiness. They don't offer all that should be taught in schools, nor do they define the extra support (interventions) which your child's teachers should share with you. Since all students have to show yearly growth, check with your child and the teacher periodically to see which standards are being taught. If the teacher says your child is not achieving as needed, ask for specific standards that trouble your child, what they do to teach them and interventions they offer and suggestions for what you can do to help.

Use the information in this guide to begin working to help your child – or considering tutoring. More introductory explanations for ***ELA standards anchors*** and ***Math conceptual categories*** are located at my website. Learn more about study skills and study groups which help children learn how to work together at home or in community centers.

With collaboration or working together, the use of standards help stakeholders to improve student growth improve each year. They offer various types of support to students with special needs and for English Language learners. More specific information is located online at the CCSS site. More information on what you can do to prepare your child your child at home for school success is located in Part III of this guide. .

English/Language Arts and Literacy

The school subject, English/Language Arts, develops students' abilities to use written and spoken English. Literacy is the ability to read and write. It is developed through speaking and listening and language/grammar in addition to researching, observing, thinking and communicating. Most of these are skills that you introduce at home.

The four ***College and Career Readiness (CCR) anchor standards*** in English/Language Arts and Literacy give important knowledge and skills based in literacy:

Reading, Writing, Speaking and Listening and Language

Deeper learning with higher order thinking skills for greater understanding is carried out through the English/Language Arts anchors and literacy skills with non-fiction content in

History, Social Studies, Science and Technical Subjects.

They represent the next generation of K-12 standards by offering a vision of what it means to be literate and prepared for future success.

CCS ELA and Literacy standards are different from past standards in the following ways.

- They focus on complex (harder) books and reading materials, use academic vocabulary (look up terms in dictionaries) using language from reports and documents used in the real world.
- They use evidence from texts and readings to learn new information and new ways of using it, not just use what students may already know or experienced in social studies, science and other subjects. They do this by defending claims (tell why certain things were chosen), getting others to change (use persuasion), careful analyses (thinking to figure out) and taking time to really look at or examine issues.
- They use nonfiction texts that real businesses use as content, plus use literature about diverse groups, so students can learn more about our world and how to operate alone and in groups of different people.

Standards are for each grade, and in grade 6 teachers use their content area expertise to teach literacy in course subjects. Students will:

- read stories and literature from different cultures and time periods;
- read harder or more complex documents with facts and background explanations in real world documents for science, social studies, etc.;
- answer harder or challenging questions that push them to use what they read (not just what they know already) for critical thinking, problem solving, and skills for after graduation success.

Assessments for test guides for each state are available. [11] Definitions of the four English/Language Arts and Literacy Anchors and what you can do at home to introduce the anchors follow.

Reading is the act of looking at, and understanding, the meaning of letters, words and symbols. It's a complex skill that's not naturally learned. Your child needs to develop reading habits and should like to read. You can begin the reading process before your baby is born by reading to her so she hears the soothing sounds of your voice. You'll get used to reading and it'll be easier for you to continue reading to her after birth.

Parents in the past sent their children to school to learn to read, but you need to start that process at home now. If not, your child will be behind on the first day of school. Children at school are expected to know a lot, so parents have to do a lot to prepare them for school. It's like sports – you practice until you get good at it, just as parents have to practice reading and communicating with their children until they learn the skills. These are basic skills needed by all children before they can read successfully.

You need books at home and your child needs to see you reading while children read. If you have problems reading, you can still "read" the pictures when your child is little, then you need to reach out to others for help so you learn to read better. If you have few books at home, talk to the librarian about books to borrow and buy dollar store books with good stories. There's a different feel to reading paper books rather than just reading on electronic screens, so mix it up.

Early foundational or basic skills in reading are presented grade by grade, but students can move beyond them when they become proficient. They include:

- print concepts (follow words, alphabet sequences in ABC order);
- phonological awareness (listen to sounds of words and pay attention to syllables in words);
- phonics (sounding out words);
- fluency (using many words in reading and speaking); and
- word recognition (when your child remembers what they see and can say the words or groups of words (terms).

Jump ahead in this guide to the chapter on "*What You Do At Home is More Important*" to find suggestions or clues that you can use to help your child become more capable in reading, mathematics and doing many other things. After doing those things for his age group and reading still seems challenging, get his eyes checked and check for any special needs. Then get a phonics book from the library and help him listen to sounds and words that way. Attend story time at the library where you'll learn skills to help your child. Focus on making reading a part of your home life since it's so important in learning to function at home, school and in the world.

Writing The purpose of writing is to communicate clearly so others can understand what you're saying or writing. As you speak or write you change or adapt sentence structure (form), content and the language (grammar) you use. Most toddlers learn to hold writing tools when their fingers and hand eye coordination develop. As they mature and begin seeing words that you write, they will want to mimic you so they need to see you writing and hear you talking. This is the start to connecting reading with lines drawn on paper that's used without thinking.

Later, your child will use the reading-writing connection to:

- give their views or opinions and support others' opinions;
- demonstrate understanding of school subjects, and
- clearly communicate real and imagined stories, experiences and events by linking their reading and thinking with writing.

Speaking and Listening Students need to be able to understand words before producing and using them. When little, they need to hear what is said (oral language) to improve literacy levels. Talk to your children, explain things to them, and ask questions that they can answer using more complete sentences as they mature. Children of all ages can read aloud to you which helps them understand what they read. To make reading more interesting, read with expression in your voice, then your children will learn to do the same.

Language Conventions are generally accepted standards and rules. Language is grammar which is used in formal spoken and written English (proper English). The more you read, the more you understand language. Vocabulary is used in reading, writing, speaking and listening and your child needs to use a dictionary (it's okay to carry one around) and later, use encyclopedias and other books. These help your child understand big words and more informative text used in the real world, like health reports about your city, topics from news documentaries and papers (documents) used in the workplace. Also play word games at home like Scrabble, Scrabble Slam, crossword puzzles, word search, Sudoku and others.

When students become proficient with the Common Core standards, they become ***College and Career Ready*** (CCR) literate persons who:

- show they can learn alone and with others;
- learn more about school content that connects with real life;
- understand the importance of using evidence as proof;
- communicate clearly in different situations with different people listening to them;

- concentrate and pay attention while being willing to learn new things while making wiser choices;
- understand when and how to use technology and digital media;
- understand and work with people from different cultures who have different perspectives or ideas and thoughts.

Mathematics

Mathematics is the abstract, not concrete, science of numbers and the study of patterns and exactly defined objects. To solve problems, mathematics uses processes (or steps) involving

- quantity (indefinite number amounts),
- space (with 1 dimension - like a dot on a line, 2 dimension -length and width or 3- length, width and depth) and
- their relationships (how they interact with each other).

Recent research noted that U.S. schools had to become more focused with easier to understand math. In order to improve mathematics achievement, the math standards are clear and specific, not general.

Conceptual (something that is thought about) categories in math are major topics in mathematics. They stress understandings of key ideas and they use organizing principles like the laws of arithmetic to structure ideas.

Does the use of arithmetic take some pressure off?

Arithmetic is a branch of mathematics where numbers and relations among numbers are studied and used to solve problems. It includes numbers, measurement and numerical computation (or processes) of the most common operations, like addition (+), subtraction (-), multiplication (x), division (÷), raising to powers/finding roots (n^2). [12]

The five ***Conceptual Categories*** in Mathematics are focused on a clear set of skills and concepts. Students learn the skills and concepts during each grade and across grades. The problems needing to be solved can be taken from real world problems, not just imaginary. They include:

Numbers and Quantity, Algebra, Functions, Geometry and Statistics and Probability

In early childhood settings, math experiences concentrate on numbers: a) whole numbers; b) operations [+, -, x and ÷]; c) relations [=, > or <];

d) geometry (imagining objects or shapes out in space); and
e) measurement (figure out an amount or degree). Math is also mixed in or integrated in other school subjects during early childhood settings.

Middle and high school math standards allow students to apply mathematical ways of thinking to real issues and challenges, like those used by college students and employees. It's not required, but each middle and high school can select one of four model pathways (or math sequences) to use with their students, including:

(1) Two algebra courses and a geometry course integrated with some data, probability and statistics;
(2) An international sequence of 3 courses: numbers, algebra, geometry and probability and statistics;
(3) A condensed version of the traditional pathways where students take high school Algebra split in grades 7 and 8;
(4) A condensed version of the integrated pathways where no content is omitted with calculus or other college- level courses by 12th

College and Career Readiness (CCR) standards are found in each pathway. To build mathematic understanding, curriculum content standards used in school subjects must be connected to math assignments so students use and practice mathematics.

Mathematical Practices describe the processes of:
a) problem solving (find solutions to difficult or complex issues);
b) reasoning and proof (connections between experiences and knowledge coupled with logical arguments to reach conclusion);
c) communication (exchange of information or news);
d) connections and representation (links to math thinking tools); and
e) proficiencies (skills that students learn).

The processes and proficiencies are used to help children see math as useful and worthwhile when they work hard and believe they can do math. This is ***mathematics literacy*** which is used in everyday life and is introduced by parents and families. The standards include these changes from past standards.

- Fewer topics are used and students should understand lower math rules and foundations. They need to understand what math terms (concepts) mean and how to use math steps correctly.
- Connections to link different topics are used, with math terms that require students to think as they use math rules to solve problems.

- Harder work (rigor) with deeper understandings of math concepts and rules are needed, and they need to understand and apply them.

Mathematics is a subject that some adults find hard to perform. They may feel anxious and react to it like stage fright with resentment or panic. This is math anxiety. You may find that you feel like this, even though you use math every day at home when you shop, when measuring for recipes, when doing taxes, etc. Try to psyche yourself out. If this is a problem for you, you want to make sure that you don't pass it to your children. [13]

Talk about solving problems with things familiar to you. Use games like dominos, Sudoku and Connect Four that require mental math. Go to your local public library to find a simpler math book that breaks information down for you. Ask the librarian and she'll search for what you need while you wait! If you like the book, buy it used on line for your home library.

The nine ***Mathematics Conceptual Categories*** in all grades and branches of mathematics are defined briefly here. The first 6 categories are introduced and mastered in elementary so students can do a better job in middle and high schools. Students should be able to move to other skills when they are mastered, not just move with grade levels.

1. ***Numbers and Quantity:*** A number is a sum of units that are added; a quantity is an indefinite or unknown amount. At home, children start out by counting objects (things) and begin to learn shapes (circle, square, etc.). They should eventually be able to count 100 objects with whole numbers. They then learn to describe shapes and space (area within an unbroken set of points), but the most time should be spent on numbers.

2. ***Counting and Cardinality:*** Counting is the naming of units to find total numbers (2, 4, 6 etc.). Cardinality is a number used to mean quantity or how many (like 4 or 10), but not order (1, 2, 3 etc.). With your help, children can learn how many or what comes 1st, 2nd, etc.

3. ***Operations and Algebraic Thinking:*** Operation is a process or action, such as addition or subtraction performed in a certain sequence or order and with rules that have to be followed. In Algebraic Thinking, you work with unknown quantities and arithmetic operations, patterns and symbols representing numbers. Addition is putting together and adding to, and subtraction is taking apart and taking from. Operations in math are actions which produce a new value from one or more input values: 1 + 2 are inputs; =3 is new value.

4. ***Numbers and Operations in Base 10:*** A base is a way to express numbers using place value with columns. Base 10 is worth 10 times the amount in another column. This is like 12 cents is worth 1 dime (which is the same as 10 cents) plus 2 cents.

5. ***Measurement and Data:*** Measurement is a unit in a system used to figure quantity or the amount or number of something. Data are facts that are used to draw conclusions. Teach children to measure the length (how long) and width (how wide) of objects and compare them.

6. ***Geometry*** is the mathematics of shapes, and it uses relationships and properties or math rules. It deals with points, lines, shapes and space. Plane geometry uses flat shapes or 2 dimensional (2D) lines, circles and triangles. Solid Geometry uses solid or 3 dimensional (3D) shapes like cubes and spheres. Children can then describe shapes and space (area within an unbroken set of points) as they understand math rules.

7. ***Algebra*** uses numbers and letters (or symbols) that represent numbers. You can practice algebra on a multiplication table while figuring out unknown numbers.

8. ***Functions*** are special relationships between values. It always has three parts: the input, relationship and output (related to the input). Functions are written as f(x).

9. ***Statistics and Probability*** deal with numerical data. ***Statistics*** is the study of data, from its collection to analysis and presentation. ***Probability*** is a chance of something happening.

Practicing math is like practicing a sport. Look for the use of math in everyday situations with your child so you both feel at ease with its use.

1. It becomes a habit when you practice it enough (you persevere) to make sense of the problems you keep trying to find answers to.
2. You can figure math out in your head (mental math) while you construct questions and figure out what others are working on.
3. You can argue and critique others' reasoning, use math facts to guide your thinking and model or show your work to others.
4. You can practice math by using it strategically with a plan and the appropriate tools (calculators, rulers, etc.) while checking your answers to make sure they're exact and correct.

Teaching [children]…what counts is best. -- *Bob Talber*

PART III

Clues to Link Home and School

If my mind can conceive it,
and my heart can believe it
– then I can achieve it. – *Jesse Jackson*

This part of the guide offers practical information and strategies as clues that you can try at home with your children as they grow and develop from infancy through high school graduation. Some families may think they're going the "wrong way" or they feel clueless in their actions as they work to make a difference. What one family does may be considered the wrong way, but another family doing almost the same thing may get different results. There are many variables involved because families and each of us are diverse with our own way of doing things. Each action we take is like a puzzle piece with some pieces that fit and some that don't.

This guide offers clues to working through some of the puzzles in family actions. A clue can be something physical, like a guide that points the way to a solid piece of information that can lead to knowledge or a discovery. A clue is usually part of a list of things that can lead to unknown solutions since most people put their own spin on decisions they make.

The home preparations in this guide and the offered clues can help you link home with school more easily as your children grow and develop. These clues offer possibilities or reminders for wellness as you actively conduct activities that help you make decisions for a healthy and fulfilling life. With these clues you can help improve the well-being of your family to become more healthy, happy, prosperous and/or successful as you empower yourself and your family.

I discovered that success is not a mystery; it leaves clues every step of the way.... Winners do things losers don't want to do. People who make it across the finish line have a different mode of thinking from those who don't. – *Dr. Phil*

10. Your Demographic Status Influences Success, but…

Where you live, the job you hold, the education you've had, the school your children attend, healthcare you receive and foods your family eat are statistical data collected for use in our national census. The census provides reliable up-to-date statistical information for making forecasts so government can plan better services and solve problems to improve the quality of our lives. This data is used to possibly and eventually solve future issues that can impact the academic achievement of your children.

In the same way, this guide can assist you and your family in making plans that can help you improve and rejuvenate the quality of your home life as you prepare your children to achieve academically. Both the government and you use demographic information to develop better future plans. [14]

<u>Demographic</u> human factors demonstrate our diversity through biological and environmental differences that separate and distinguish individuals and groups. <u>Biological features</u> of diversity include age, ethnicity, gender, race (perceived physical differences) and our physical and mental abilities. <u>Environmental features</u> help shape individuals because of their experiences like education, family status, culture or way of life, communication style, religion, first language, birth order, income, work experience, military experience and geographic locations.

We have different lifestyles, traditions and perspectives, sometimes due to our cultures, and it can influence and shape how we communicate, view conflict, define, solve and resolve problems. An <u>influence</u> is the capacity or power to be a compelling force on or producer of effects on the actions, behaviors or opinions of others. Certain things <u>influence, but don't predict</u> outcomes that will happen when a child enters school. Families, teachers and other students are important influencers with children. Following are other things that influence the academic achievement and quality of well-being of our children.

Some researchers, educators and other people believe that a person's economic level or race <u>determines</u> whether they will learn or not and how they will treat them. They may not do this intentionally, but it happens. When looking at a <u>family's income</u>, some people believe that low-income parents do not give children experiences that open their worlds and build their communication skills. During this period of the shrinking middle class, more students are thrust into lower income situations and more contradictions will grow. When families with higher incomes do little to help their children develop and learn, the same can happen, and income, alone, doesn't tell the complete story. Many educators and Americans, in general, feel more comfortable in talking about the economic levels of students rather than race and ethnicity.

In fact, some feel that we've moved beyond racial issues - possibly so they don't have to acknowledge or discuss them at all?! When data is reviewed, race is still a factor. Race is hard for most Americans to talk about because of societal reasons and internal barriers (Sue, 2014). [15] We try to be polite, we think that if we see color it means you are biased, or we don't want to show emotion. We also don't want to acknowledge privilege nor the fact that we are prejudiced. We are all racial and cultural beings with identities that vary according to where we stand at a certain time. [16]

When we don't talk about issues their effects still remain with us. Other influencers on your child cut across all family incomes and race. Some of these influencers are unspoken topics that we may think about, but don't voice. They are sensitive issues - private to a degree, but they can influence our children's development and academic achievement.

Family composition is important. Children with only one parent involved in their lives can suffer, some children more than others. When looking at the statistics, 1 in 5 American mothers of all income levels and education have multiple children with different fathers. [17] This is a complex situation since the single parent has to plan and co-parent with the input of multiple fathers, if they are in the children's lives. In 2013, 62% of households headed by single women were European American, 30% were African American and 8% were other. [18] Census data is inadequate for measuring complex family structures like single parents today who may adopt alternative and flexible living arrangements.

Children living with one parent are more likely to live in poverty, develop behavioral problems and are more exposed to abuse, especially from live-in friends of the single parent. Many girls who grow up without a father may grow up too quickly, and boys may show antisocial behavior to hide the fact that they want a father. When children grow up with a mother who may be absent physically or emotionally, they can suffer long term damage to self-esteem, guilt for thinking they're the reason for the mother's leaving, trust issues with other adults, trouble building relationships and possibly a lifetime of grieving in various ways.

When parents are present, but uninvolved or neglectful, problems also occur. These parents are consumed with their own needs for various reasons, and neglect to raise their children. They may allow their children to do as they please, they are friends rather than parents, they have few rules and do not provide structure for healthy emotional development. They shift most responsibilities on to older children or grandparents or assume that schools or groups will take care of them. Their children can be lonely with little love and social skills, and they are apt to be emotionally, physically and emotionally disconnected from people. They can also have academic and behavioral problems. This may make it hard to find and keep jobs and they may have legal troubles. [19]

When children are involved too early in sexual matters they are placed at risk. They can experience psychological problems and more abuse with antisocial activity like drug use and more sexual activity. These behaviors can impact learning with academic problems and lowered education aspirations where they are not interested in future education plans. The media and lax family situations can influence our children's sexuality.

Another sensitive issue is how your children see their bodies or body image. [20] A possible issue for girls and boys, body image and appearance can relate to weight, skin color, health issues and other physical attributes. Most people in our nation are prejudiced and their perceptions and reactions about body image, including how you view your child, can be hurtful. It's influenced by the media and for some, it's seen as a personal failure and can lower self-worth. Poor body image can be linked to diminished mental performance, low self-esteem, anxiety and depression.

Though not a sensitive issue, recent research on sleep points to the fact that many adults and their children are not getting enough. Consequences for not getting enough sleep can include increased risk of unintentional injuries and death, low grades and poor school performance, negative moods and increased likelihood of stimulant use.

Some of the above information is collected for census data and some of it indicates whether children have the support they need to grow and develop healthily. Healthy family situations can influence the achievement gap.

***I've learned that our background and circumstances may have influenced who we are, but we are responsible for who we become.** –Author Unknown*

11. What You Do At Home Is More Important!

Interactions with your family environment can be more important to your children's development than demographic information as used in the census. It's more important than child care, how much money you make and some aspects of schooling. These interactions can help children develop different and improved sets of skills and behaviors that align or match with academic achievement and learning more about life. Some believe that the achievement gap may begin when infants and toddlers grow up with certain home influencers and continues through high school graduation. The previous chapter introduced influencers, and this chapter will note some clues as to what you can do.

Family patterns and approaches. Adults and children go through periods of development, or patterns of change, that begin at birth and continue throughout life. Certain developmental skills are important for later learning, and children usually display them if they don't have special needs. [21] Some of the first skills occur naturally as infants and toddlers grow and change, and it's important that parents encourage and support their development in the building of skills in the following areas:

- physically with gross motor (using large muscles like crawling) and fine motor (using small muscles by using fingers);
- cognitively, with learning and problem solving skills;
- socially and emotionally, to interact in positive ways with others while developing their own personalities (children begin learning to help themselves about seven months of age); and
- speech and communication skills which help them speak, use and understand written language to communicate when they're older.

Patterns are actions that are repeated over time and can provide support and encouragement to your children. Important patterns occur at the same time through balancing love and nurturing, stability without too many major changes and clear communication. Your children are with you for only a couple of decades, and they deserve the best beginnings with you as their first teachers. They can then help you later in life.

Your parenting style is very important. [22] When parents intentionally use opportunities to teach their children about life, they talk to them about a lot of things and build communication skills. Children respond to parents' questions which builds their confidence and classroom skills.

Some parents prefer a more natural approach where they let children play all the time. In his approach, parents don't talk to their children much, and when they do it's to discipline them with little shared communication. Children know who runs the family since parents are in control and they learn self-sufficiency by learning to do things themselves. A down side to the natural approach is your children may not do as well in school since they may not communicate well and don't have confidence skills.

It's best to blend the opportunities approach with the natural approach. With the blended approach you share communication and learning skills while teaching your children self-sufficiency skills. Your home life will be more creative and full of life and your children will understand that you value learning. You and your children will enjoy each other better and you'll possibly more easily meet the *Tough Questions* challenges.

Another approach that blends the two previous ones is democratic, positive or conscious parenting. When you parent democratically you equally respect all people in the family, no matter the age, and children grow up understanding responsibility. Everyone has a voice, though parents have the last say so that everyone has to accept. With conscious parenting, you choose to give your children quality feedback about how to respond in life. They discuss rules so children understand why they are needed and children are given choices at times with an understanding of consequences which helps them to think with deductive reasoning. Parents praise children for working together for the good of the family. Acceptance, understanding and confidence happen with this view and your children can easily become leaders since they see democracy in action.

Gender. No matter how you parent, make sure that you don't treat your daughter or son differently because of gender. Strive to make both of them able to perform well so they are capable of doing a lot of things. They'll think more, be creative and more positive, not as bored or whiny. They will be well-rounded and more content with themselves and with you. Developmentally, girls can be more verbal, coordinated and considered as helpless and boys can be more physical and prone to leadership and considered as having power. Parental efforts can balance these attributes.

Boys and girls both go through periods of liking their same sex more and being rejected by the other sex, which is also done with other factors like religion or race. By mid to late elementary, boys and girls start interacting more and when puberty strikes (from 10 – 18) they may begin to have romantic thoughts. When children have high levels of social and emotional competence, love with good parenting and academic success, they are more apt to not join violence related or early sexual activities.

Family composition. In the beginning may be a far cry from what actually is, since you already may be parents if you're reading this book. A good message before becoming sexually active and one that you can possibly pass on to your older children: be proactive when they first begin developing a relationship to lessen reacting later. Take four or more months to get to know the prospect better before being intimate. Look for clues about whether that person would be good parent material, or not. Then determine if you need to stay together or break up before possible pregnancy or disease occurs. Everything and nothing is 100%!

It's harder on some children than others when brought up in single parent households. They can get beyond the loss or missing them, but it doesn't happen by never talking about the missing parent. You and your children may possibly need extra help from helping professionals or groups to help you deal with this. [23] No matter your home life, remember to keep your children safe from other adults you bring into your home, no matter their gender. You can find organizations supporting both parents in each state, [24] plus view videos, [25] learn more about children with incarcerated parents [26] and/or find initiatives [27] in your area that see the need for both fathers and mothers to be in their children's lives.

Culture and healthy racial identity. Your family's culture and your racial identity are important. [28] Your children's self-acceptance, confidence and self-awareness are connected to how you deal with difference. Children begin to make judgments about people based on what they hear and see from their families, media images and any segregated home and community environments. If you display prejudged opinions or bias and put down people who look like your children, they feel your bias, too. This can form insecurities that may take a lifetime to get over.

Children from the ages of 3-6 are curious, independent, focused at times and they like to learn. They are too young to intellectually understand complex issues, but they become aware of differences and similarities around race, culture, physical differences, disabilities and gender. You want your children to feel comfortable around others in child care, school, friendships or other situations. If we build relationships with others we can work towards collaboration and peace.

Test yourself for hidden biases, [29] and use a parent guide for discussing racial identity. [30] Then introduce healthy racial identity to children when they're toddlers or at any age - even to yourself as an adult - so it becomes a natural part of living. Websites will help you understand more about raising bi-racial children from a mother's point of view, adopted children and biracial children's point of view. [31]

Body image and wellness. The mind-body connection is important since good foods help fuel our bodies and our brains, and along with movement, they work together to influence how we feel about ourselves. As adults, we have a tendency to overlook our health – especially if it relates to our eating habits that may make us feel better. If you had a choice, which would you prefer – working on your body's health so your child picks up good habits or allowing him to eat a lot of unhealthy foods and exercise little so he gets old folks diseases when he's still young. (I recently read about a 3 year old with diabetes). You choose.

You may want to consider changing your lifestyle while you rejuvenate your family to start new habits for life! You want to begin habits that will start and keep your babies and older children on the path to wellness. At the same time you want them, and you, to feel good about yourselves on that particular journey so: be positive, use self-talk when you see negative things in the media; don't emphasize numbers but how you feel; stop comparing yourself to others; spend time with others working to improve; move and enjoy your body as you take care of yourself and your family.

Healthy foods are cheaper than fast and convenience foods when you look at what you get for your money and the returns on your health. Learn more about reading food labels, [32] not eating GMOs (genetically modified organisms put into foods that are not healthy and children may be allergic to them), cooking at home and growing a small vegetable or herb garden. Share these activities with your family while you read to learn more about eating healthily. Plan and organize meal-times so cooking takes less time and it becomes family time to enjoy with each other. [33] Watch food shows with healthy cooking together. Many of us eat foods good for our souls that remind us of home, but when we eat it a lot, we have to beware. Watch the Soul Food Junkie documentary [34] for another view of our comfort foods. Then hold your own nutritious cook-off! [35]

Body image around weight depends on affordable healthcare, access to nutritious foods, wellness and safe places to move our bodies. You want to break bad habits as you change your eating to live a different lifestyle! [36]. A three minute video on obesity [37] information can help you make sense about why the average weight of so many Americans is higher than most people in the world. Changing our lifestyles with eating in mind brings other issues to the forefront since it's a complex issue. [38]

Screen time and sleep. Screen time is hurting our children and family relationships! Screens are any electronic devices with screens like televisions, computers, digital games, cell phones, etc. Too much time spent in front of screens can affect our brains, hand and eye coordination, plus it takes too much time away from the human need of socialization for learning, playing and talking with others. Old and young get addicted! [39]

Parents have a false sense of security when you assume that your children stay on the waves you program. When they have access to adult topics due to screen time and other issues, children (even up to high school) are too young to have the skills to make wise decisions. This is not good for their development nor your family.

You've seen children old before their time – and sometimes this is acted out in abusive situations with adults. Make sure that your children are too busy to experiment with sex, drugs or other bad influences that are definitely not appropriate if they live with you. Know your child's friends, their families and who they communicate with online. Don't assume and don't let bad habits start or continue.

Sleep is another area that may possibly need your attention on the journey to wellness and moving beyond influencers. New research is out on the need for sleep – by adults, even! [40] Early bedtime for children gives adults more time to unwind, reflect and rejuvenate for the next day, plus it's good for their brain and body growth. Make sure your toddler gets from eight to ten hours of sleep every night plus naps during the day. Older children need at least 8 hours of sleep nightly, even into their late teens. Adults need at least 7 hours of sleep nightly for brain and bodily health for the next day. All of us need to sleep sounder and dream!

Family safety and security are up to us also! In these sometimes perilous times, we hope and pray that our children remain safe when they are not physically with us. We have to talk with them about thinking before acting, no matter where they are. [41] We have to be proactive, making sure that certain things are in place before trouble knocks at our doors. When you are in need of another kind of protection in the form of professional services, you have help in planning for the future while you protect your identity, so you can "Worry Less and Live More." [42]

Choose to let it go. Whatever the "it" is, it can possibly keep you from expressing your pain and admitting your responsibility. Or it can keep you from forgiving yourself or others, if needed. When you let it go, you can stop blaming others; focus on the present, your family and your job; then forgive whoever or whatever, and yourself. By doing this, you free yourself to create what you want in your family with positive attitudes, effort and planning. Believe that you can make positive differences in your family, even though it may take a while!

Choose hope: Another influencer is how you feel about the future. When you can't let go of recent or multigenerational pain or trauma, it shapes your children's development, academic achievement and their view of the world. The past cannot be changed, and if you cling to it you can get stuck in it and feel powerless, angry, hurt and victimized. Find out how to put forgiveness and joy into your life as you move beyond barriers that may have been built when you were young.

Don't sabotage good things that are happening because you think that you don't deserve them or you may feel disloyal to past friends because you're making different choices now. Use your journal as you go through the change and let your faith guide you.

You have to look deeper, way below the anger, the hurt, the hate, the jealousy, the self-pity, way down deeper where the dreams lie, son [and daughter]. Find your dream. It's the pursuit of the dream that heals you.

-Billy Mills, Oglala Lakota

The following clues in this part of the book will help you and your children on your family's journey to link learning at home with academic achievement at school. Together with many other clues throughout this guide, you and your significant other will feel more confident that you indeed are your children's best teachers. In this section, you will see standards written in *italics.*

Parents have become so convinced that educators know what is best for their children that they forget that they themselves are really [or can be] the experts. *–Marian Wright Edelman*

Birth, Pre-school and Kindergarten

If you want to know the end, look at the beginning
-African Proverb

What You Observe

- *My baby seems pretty alert, but I want to make sure that I'm doing what's best to prepare him for learning.*
- *Your child seems different when comparing her to others.*
- *Should I be concerned about reading when he is so young?*

How You Can Help
The first six years of life are very important to children's future lives in that their future health, growth and development, happiness and school achievement begin with the family. Doing your best with your birth through kindergarten age children is especially important since children learn more quickly than at any other time in life.

As parents, no matter where you are in your life and development, you want to give your children the best beginnings. If you are in a negative situation, you don't want your children to possibly pick up habits that may lead them there. We owe the best of nurturing and our time to our children so they have better chances and this book may guide you to where you want and need to be.

Children's brains develop with love and nurturing or an upbringing that gives them what they need. Nurturing can affect future learning skills and social and emotional abilities. Nurturing helps your babies and children develop trust and security that later becomes confidence. At the same time, children from one – three years of age need to be given chances to make some choices and decisions so they learn to be independent. They do this as they become more mobile and learn to walk, become curious about their environment and start learning how to manipulate things they come into contact with. If parents keep toddlers dependent, they may start to feel shame and to doubt their own abilities. So watch yourself!

Try to choose child care arrangements with the best quality that you can afford. If they emphasize and do social and emotional growth and learning, that's quality. To take advantage of brain growth during this period child care should offer experiences to help children build skills, not play all day. This helps children grow up into healthy, caring, capable and responsible adults who can contribute to their future families, communities and nation. Look for safety, happiness and nurturing when you go to visit day cares. Be diligent and also investigate in-home child care if you use it. Check to see if your state offers assistance, if needed.

Don't rely on day care to teach your child. That's your job! It takes time and effort - but you can do it. Be sensitive to your children who may be in child care for long hours, or when you spend too much time in your possible addiction to screen time. Watch your child's social skills, especially if she is in day care. Take the time to teach her how to interact respectfully with other children and adults: to share, take turns and follow rules as preparation for kindergarten. Make time for your toddler to socialize at times with children of the same age, if not in day care. Other ways or clues to help your children follow:

1. Nurture your baby and yourself before birth and minimize stress in your life by learning to relax. If you decide to breastfeed, you have an automatic stress reliever and the best beginnings. [43]
2. Spend time without technology at times and listen to nature: talk and read to her, sing, hug and cuddle. Strive for peace for you and home.
3. Limit time in the playpen when toddlers want to be mobile but safe.
4. Caring, nutrition, stimulation and talking to your child are needed from birth throughout life. Read more to find things to talk about.
5. Let your baby safely explore objects with different textures in various situations as they show their curiosity; use physical movement; and listen to soft music.
6. Take walks with your family and hold your baby so he sees what you see and talk to him about it. Read, if needed, to learn more so you have plenty to say about what you see. Enjoy this time away from screens!
7. Make sure your toddler gets from eight to ten hours of sleep plus naps.
8. When your child has a temper tantrum, rather than just punishment, try to figure out the underlying problem. This helps him begin to understand his feelings, and later with vocabulary he can express himself in constructive ways.

- When you discipline your children, try time out for your toddler with one minute for each year of age. Kneel down to her eye level to briefly explain the behavior that was inappropriate. When older, have them explain to you what they did. If you spank children for putting themselves in danger, get them used to only one or two licks. As they mature, you won't have to do much more than that, with talking.

9. Minimize loud music, negative behaviors, junk foods, chemical scents.
10. When you cook, let your child measure, pour & compare with recipes.
11. Understand that each child is an individual and learning differences occur, even within your own family. [44]
12. An early way to build trust: create a goodbye routine for babies, don't put too much emphasis on change. Stay calm, say goodbye, leave.
13. When you praise children, praise their processes (hard work, sticking to the problem until solved, learning from mistakes and showing improvement) not just talent, prettiness or ability.
14. Don't laugh at bad behavior, it's not cute, especially as she gets older!
15. "Make do" and be creative with substitutions like playing with boxes.
16. Don't feel guilty! If you are a working parent, and you need help, ask! Trade free time with another parent while she watches your children at times, or hire someone. You'll have more time to follow book clues!
17. Relax and enjoy each other's company when sharing in chores or play.
18. Reading must be started before kindergarten by parents. It's not something that children do unless they see others doing it. Find books with pictures that look like your family. Hold family readings.
19. Read ads on boxes and television to him so he sees links between real words and heard sounds.
20. Talk to your baby so she learns skills like speaking, learns how to listen, focuses on objects when observing them, and able to explain to you her ideas. *This is literacy.*
21. When you do activities with your toddler, tell him what you're doing to help build language skills. Teach the alphabet song, show your child the letters in her name. Make labels for items in the home. When you watch shows together, ask questions and he can explain to you. Make communication a natural part of our day.
22. With preschoolers, play rhyming games, talk to them about what you're doing, take trips to the library, read at least 30 minutes daily – breaking it up - and ask questions. Sit down to eat dinner sometimes.

Do the difficult things while they are easy and do the great things while they are small. A journey of a thousand miles must begin with a single step. *–Lao Tzu*

Elementary: Primary (1st, 2nd and 3rd Grades)

What You Observe

- *Your child reads well, but you know she can do better.*
- *Your child is alone around groups of other children and doesn't seem to get along with them.*
- *Your child has become the class clown.*

How You Can Help

Plan for Third Grade early since your extra support will be needed! Third grade is a transition year since it's the last year of primary school and teachers expect children to take more responsibility for their learning. If your child had a solid foundation from the earlier grades, he will do well with encouragement and your extra support.

It's also a time when peer relationships become important. Students need to be able to speak out when called on in class, even though they sometimes don't like to take the risk of being called out by their teachers in front of classmates. Practice speaking out and asking for help with her. She likes to conform to her peers and they may kid her for doing things different, and that's okay. Talk about being different and not following the crowd if actions are against your family values. Get her used to doing things differently. If he has become the class clown, look for deeper issues like anxiety or stress – is something different and stressful going on at home? Are other things happening that are different? Ask her!

By this age, your child needs to know how to manage disappointments and frustrations in acceptable ways to help with social and emotional development. Help him deal with peer pressure by being in a different environment: find a community group with educational functions or form your own study group for friends with similar hobbies or interests.

In Language Arts/English, students are expected to read with confidence and figure out information by thinking through word problems. Reading gets more challenging and vocabulary words are tougher. In early grades, science and history or social studies are integrated into math and reading, but now they will begin as stand-alone subjects. In Mathematics, students need to memorize and understand complex thinking. The study/ fun group will come in handy for building skills together with a group. Look for educational fun things to do. Make learning positive in your household.

Second and third grades is the time that parents have to step up since your extra support is needed. You need to show a positive attitude and enthusiasm about school and what he's doing. Talk about your high expectations and set clear boundaries without value judgments on some issues. Show your patience and develop a manageable routine so you have time to help with homework, along with actively listening to him. When you actively listen, get down on her level so you can give feedback, give your full attention with eye contact, nod your head and encourage talk. Other clues for learning at home follow.

1. Read to your child, and have your child read to you. Ask questions about what he reads and explain answers to you. Get him to focus on paper books, not just screens. Do this daily.

- By now your child should be reading since it's very important at this stage. Use library programs for extra reading support. Be creative and get your child to tell stories, write them down and read them to you.
- Make sure she sees adults reading at home. If you need to read better, learn how at the public library or in an adult education class.
- Make sure that your child reads some books that have children from your culture in them and make sure that she has skills that lead to fair minded thinking. [45]

2. Watch your child play and display social skills: does she listen and play well with others? Is he independent, flexible, and sharing? Does she value differences in her playmates? Do you? Does he like to work? Does he show empathy, caring and respect? Model it!
3. When needed speak up or advocate for your child by showing support.
4. Open up your child's world together: go outside to play, discover free exhibits at your public library and museums; take nature walks, talk and get books about what you see, hear, feel, smell, touch.
5. If your family members do not speak and read English, you can still learn literacy skills together. Tell stories, read picture books, say rhymes and sing songs; visit the public library often; engage in meaningful conversations; watch educational programs together and talk to each other. *English Language Learners*
6. Get a child's dictionary (new or used) so your child learns definitions of big words. Make vocabulary learning a game: be creative! When she asks questions, use books to find answers. Start a library of used

books and a set of encyclopedias at home to show you value learning. Use them to look up answers when questions arise.

7. Make sure he uses his imagination, art and science when playing at times with non-electronic toys and books.
8. A few chores need to be done around the house so your child knows she is capable and can do a good job with that and with school.
9. Make sure she gets 8 or more hours of sleep every day.
10. Your child should know how to whisper, follow directions, be confident and ask for help by now. If not, teach him.
11. Begin to learn the multiplication table and math facts.
12. Organization is important: make a study location without distractions. Put a family calendar on the refrigerator with due dates and schedules for school meetings, family activities and assignments. Plan big projects so deadlines are met.
13. Eat healthily, move and exercise as a family and limit technology use.
14. Your child's happiness or lack of it should not control your home.
15. Allow age appropriate media and don't rush your children to grow up.
16. If your child has too much stuff (toys, technology, etc.), it may be hard to be creative, curious and pretend. Let her choose what to donate.
17. Look for ways that numbers are used, and talk with your child about how you use math daily. This is *Mathematics Literacy.*
18. When you discipline, get children used to only one or two infrequent "licks" if you do that. Take more time to talk about the mistake that was made. They can start writing problems down or drawing pictures about what she needs to do to remind her not to do it again.
19. Continue to plan family time together a few times a week. Play games, try crafts, eat dinner at the table and talk, go outside and enjoy each other's company! Let children be the leaders sometimes.
20. Pay attention: by now you should know if your child has special needs, where you can get help and what you can do to help.
21. Purchase and use the *Reader's Handbook: A Student Guide for Reading and Learning* (2002, Great Source). This is a good reading resource that helps students (grades 3-12) read and understand textbooks in all subjects, for different grade levels.
22. If you have questions about your child, use a search engine but consider the source, ask your pediatrician or get books from library.

23. Did you know that some children lose knowledge during the summer because they are not learning and thinking enough? During summer breaks, enjoy your time, but make sure that children, and you, continue reading and learning. Make visiting museums fun and learning a natural part of whatever you do all year.
24. Get to know your family's extended families so children can know their relatives. They may offer clues as to why you do certain things.
25. Remember that being different is not bad. Talk about that statement with your children and make sure your children know their culture.
26. Look at family activities related to school subjects and talk about them with your children so learning becomes natural and enjoyable.
27. Help your child deal with worrying news stories.
28. Talk to her about her dreams about her future. What are her favorite programs? What kind of life does she want to live, and why? Teach her how to make plans and record in the journal.
29. Teach him how to ask for help, when needed.
30. Begin budgeting and saving for college or training after graduation.

Here's to the kids who are different...
For when they have grown,
As history's shown,
It's their difference that makes them unique. – *Digby Wolfe*

Elementary Intermediate (4th and 5th Grades)

What You Observe

- *My child acts okay at home, but seems to get in trouble more than in primary school.*
- *I wonder if my child is ready for middle school or is growing up too quickly.*
- *I don't want my child to follow negative influences, even though negatives are, unfortunately, a part of my family.*

How You Can Help

As a parent of children in the last years of elementary school, you may find that your skill levels need to increase. [46] Re-read the intro to the *Elementary Primary* chapter since it's an intro to this one.

Fourth grade is where "learning to read" changes to "reading to learn." Learn more about tutoring and what you can do to help yourself help your child. Fifth grade is the last year of elementary school, and your child has made gains in academics, growth spurts and the beginnings of hormone surges. Don't let your child's possible negative attitude bother you. Don't be pulled into whining and complaining by arguing with her. Check yourself to see if you model those behaviors.

Talk about your expectations, the differences between being positive and negative, and choices they make. If she is disrespectful, it may be a cover for not feeling okay about something. Ask your child questions and expect respectful answers while she watches body language! [47] Your child may feel confident, but watch out for the changes that are coming! Fourth grade is a good time to start family meetings. [48] They help you build stronger families as your children get older!

If your child talks about boredom at school, it may be because he's not being challenged or motivated. It could be he doesn't like the topic or there's too much desk time. It may be that he doesn't feel socially accepted and comfortable with peers, or he may not have the necessary skills for what they're doing. Talk to your child to find out what he may mean about boredom and how he needs to handle the situation, rather than just complain. Talk to the teacher if needed, using clues from *Chapter 15.*

Organization is very important in fifth grade and beyond, especially if your child is not turning in homework when you know he did it! Help him organize notebooks for each class by buying pocket folders with prongs down the middle. Require your child to bring all pocket notebooks home each day, even if there's no homework, especially if problems arise.

1. Put notebook paper in the center and put name, class, location, etc. on the cover page. Each day, date the top of the page, write notes of what happens in class and write down the homework that's assigned. [49]
2. Place graded papers in the pocket on the left and on the right place due papers and assignments that should be turned in. Label as reminders.
3. When problems occur, talk with the teacher and ask her to sign the notebook for a week at a time, or more when needed as a checking tool

4. Daily, look at the notebook, discuss the work, then sign and date it so the teacher knows you reviewed his work. This can make a big difference but you have to take time to check it daily.

If you haven't already, you may want to consider purchasing *Reader's Handbook: A Student Guide for Reading and Learning.* This is a good reading resource that helps students (grades 3-12) read and understand textbooks in all subjects, for different grade levels (elementary, middle and high). Buy it used and keep it as a reference book. It's even good for parents to review their reading skills if you're going back to school or trying to learn more to help your child with homework. [50]

Middle School Preparations. Middle school is a new experience waiting to be discovered by you and your adolescent child. With this new experience, your child may be excited. As she prepares for middle school, help her deal with the unknown by following the following clues. Initially, make sure that she becomes familiar with a combination lock.

Learn how your middle school operates. Are there teams of teachers? Do students have a different teacher for each subject? How does the school communicate with parents? Are homework and major assignments posted online or placed in the parent handbook? If you've heard rumors about the school, find the facts by talking with the principal. The summer before, find books at the library about middle school student topics. [51]

Get a middle school mascot t-shirt or car sign the spring before school starts. You may meet other parents or students by displaying the school mascot or insignia. More extracurricular activities are offered after school or in the community for this age group. Talk about interests or what they want to learn. Then sign up and try to stay until completed!

You have noticed by now that your child seems to be in between grade level development issues, but changes may occur sooner rather than later and you want to be prepared. So read the section that introduces *Middle School* also. Unless your child is in a K-8 school, you may also find that the chapter on *Selecting Schools* will be useful as you choose the middle school your child will attend – if you have choices in that matter.

1. By now your child should know how to whisper, follow directions, be confident and ask for help.
2. When you praise children, don't just praise them for talent, beauty, intelligence or abilities. It's best to praise what they are doing, like

hard work, trying many strategies, focus, perseverance or sticking to it, learning from mistakes and improvements you see.

3. Find more positive families in your area or a program that deals with academic achievement. Possibly start a study group for children to learn from each other. [52] *Relationship-building*

4. Learn more about higher-level mathematics by getting a good, easy to read book that explains math in a format simple enough for you so you can better help your children. [53]

- Learn about personal finances and math lessons for life to see how your family uses math every day. [54]
- Get over your math fears so that your child doesn't fear math.

5. Do the above with science and social studies! Encourage science explorations in the community or when traveling. Work on science fair projects each year. After it's complete, tell her to practice by explaining her project to you. For social studies, learn to use a map and take walking and riding tours of your city.

6. Make sure your child gets enough sleep, about 8 hours daily.

7. If sports take too much time from homework, consider a different sport and/or schedule time for both. Or just be realistic about your child and take him out until grades, etc. improve. You have control.

8. Organize homework space and time, set goals and use checklists. Make sure that she brings papers home in pocket notebooks.

9. Keep a family calendar on the refrigerator. Write project and assignment due dates, athletic events, and family activities on it.

10. Make sure your child keeps up with what's going on in class. Help her understand that concepts or things they talk about in class connect with other concepts. [55]

11. Children need to think, and with your help they can believe that thinking is fun while wanting to be good at it. [56]

- Get your child in the habit of talking about her thinking at times. She can write thoughts on her plans for the future in her journal, and share them with you, along with things that can get in the way. Planning now means that she may think before acting out hurtful behaviors.

12. Talk with your child about the world and growing up. Discuss current events if its age appropriate and talk about links with the past and present. *Civic literacy*

13. Actively listen to your child (and your spouse) by doing more than just hearing! Take time to stop talking and listen, then show that you heard what was said by repeating what they said or need you to do. Listen to what's being said and also to what is not said as you observe body language. Parents can figure out a lot with this skill.
14. When you discipline your child for a serious mistake, get her to write out what she did wrong, step by step; problems caused by her choices; then list choices that could have been made. She should then report that information to you. [57]
15. Make sure that your children don't get involved in adult issues. Set necessary boundaries and make sure they are respected.
16. When you talk, at times note audience (who you are talking to), persuasion (convince someone); and sequences (steps). *Literacy*
17. Help your child develop a strong vocabulary so buy and use an intermediate dictionary and he can express himself or talk more. Discussing topics with you will give him ideas to write about. *Language*

18. Be proactive by doing things before they are actually needed, so read and discuss fiction and non-fiction books about middle school now.
19. Talk to her about being cautious and paying attention to her surroundings, not scared.
20. Learn more about English Learner (EL) services at your child's school if English is not your family's first language.
21. Garden and recycle with your family. *Environmental Literacy*
22. Check state laws to see if your children are mature enough to stay alone safely at home without adult supervision. [58]
23. Use logical consequences [59] when misbehavior occurs. Figure out solutions to problems so that the misbehavior isn't repeated often.
24. Have sit-down meals at the table without electronic screens + no TV, and take this time to share. Make sure your children know dining etiquette and can use forks, knives and spoons correctly.
25. Make sure she acts and dresses appropriately for her age. Note that your clothes are not for your children. Acting appropriately means being respectful, not mimicking bad behavior seen on the screen or possibly displayed by others. Talk about meanness, if needed.
26. Give your child summer responsibilities that help her learn needed skills for growing up, like organizational and time management skills.

27. Your family's beliefs about literacy are important to your child's learning. This includes how you interact and communicate. Share family stories and discuss behaviors and the news together.
28. Talk to him about puberty changes in the body, sexually transmitted diseases, safer sex and "waiting" when you feel its time. If you need to, visit the library together. Your child will then have someone dependable to go to when questions arise.
29. Spend little time negotiating with your children – you are the adult and they are children, not your colleagues or partners!
30. Talk to teachers before problems arise. You know your child: don't wait! Use the advice in *Chapter 15.*
31. Make sure your child does not have access to adult topics on screens.
32. Your child's bedroom is not off limits to you. Check to see what he does there. Too much stuff is available easily and you want to limit that influence. Don't send him to his room for punishment if media entertainment is there, unless you remove it. At bedtime, store screens.
33. Balance sports with learning activities by making time for both. Don't overdo sports, leaving out school work: they're "student" athletes.
34. Expect respect and listen to your child as you give advice. If you lose your temper, apologize when you're cool, then continue discussing.
35. Use a planner and get your child in the habit of writing down home and class assignment due dates there. Follow up by checking to make sure they are being written down, and assignments are turned in. Go the extra step to look at grades. Have her figure out what she can do to improve, if needed, or feel more positive about the work.
36. Learn more about preventing and relieving stress, and teach your child so you both become more resilient, able to bend when winds blow.
37. Choose to be proactive and don't pass on negative traits that may be in yourself or your family. Talk to her about these traits as she gets older. They influence your children's attitudes and behaviors, whether you do anything about them or not.
38. When you engage or involve yourself with the school, your children are more likely to achieve academically, so stay engaged even when your children don't want you around.
39. Volunteer somewhere as a family so your children learn more about the world while giving back.

When young people see themselves making a difference, they also become different. - *Grace Lee Boggs*

Middle School (6th, 7th and 8th Grades)

What You Observe

- *Two transitions (sixth and eighth grades) in three years are a lot of change; or our school configuration is different, but we still need to prepare for high school. How can I help plan for success?*
- *My child does his homework at home, but the teacher says he doesn't turn it in.*

How You Can Help

Middle school can be confusing and tough on you and your child! There are more teachers, more schedules and students from other locations, more angst and lockers! Adolescence, from preteens through young adulthood (adolescence can now last until age 35 – yikes!!!) is a time when your child may start thinking differently.

She'll become more independent, more emotional and more influenced by peer pressure. The social structure in middle school may be more cruel than elementary with mean girls and boys and friendships will change frequently. At the same time, she'll have more academic responsibility with thoughts of sexuality. They are moving towards adulthood and at the same time playing with dolls and action figures.

Hold regularly scheduled family meetings to talk about issues effecting family members. They are a good communication tool to promote harmony in the family and help parents, as well as children, deal with anger, family decision making and moral reasoning. [60]

Your children will begin to regard you as knowing little and over-protective. They will pick battles with you over things you thought were settled years before. When battles involve school issues and you are considered as not knowing enough – know that you are not alone. The school counselor is there to reach your child even when you can't, so make sure you get to know him before the school year starts.

Continue to offer support by supervising study, paying attention to social drama, developing a balance between controlling and letting go. Make sure that you don't become the "cool" parent who allows misbehavior as you try to be a friend rather than parent. Set boundaries with rules and expectations and have her deal with consequences of her actions. .

Be proactive and familiar with the online student management system at your school, if available. It is like a report card. Keep homework in the forefront of all other activities, including technology usage and sports, since homework practice gets him prepared for later. Be firm and keep on top of his grades, even when he may not want to share with you. If your child has entertainment central in the bedroom, it will be best to study in a centrally located place during that first year until you see that he is doing a good job with academics. [61]

If your child is in special classes, remember that what you do at home and with teachers is more important than the label she's given. Learn the latest information about her disability or ability and make sure you advocate for her learning – and help her begin to learn what she needs to do. Make sure that your child is also being accelerated (where learning is speeded up and she's placed in another group) in her learning, not just remediated (repeating the same thing in different ways). An A in a low level class does not mean your child is getting what he or she needs to succeed.

Your child continues to need your support, and you need to continue engaging with school. When you stop engaging, so will some adolescents! Talk with your child about the importance of working hard to learn in this transitional year since its linked to future success. If the work is too easy, give your own assignments and talk to teachers.

Do the right thing. *--Spike Lee*

Re-read the introduction to *Intermediate Elementary* as a review for this year since it was written for fifth graders older than their years. More clues to link home and school for learning and living follow.

1. Remember to put away a few dollars monthly for future college expenses, and hopefully you've used your state's matching 529 Plan [62] for college info in all states. Make sure your child's grades are good so he can qualify for scholarships and internships to help. Talk to others about what they did to pay college and training expenses.
2. Get to know all his teachers early in the year. Is there a team so you can meet all teachers at the same time? It's not too scary and will be a good use of your time! Write any questions you want answered and record responses you get since you may be nervous and you don't want to forget anything. Share this info with the other parent.
3. When problems arise, assist your child in finding solutions. Ask questions, expect answers and discuss problems and possible

solutions. Get him to research the problem on line if he has nothing to say so he can write about it in his journal. Discuss what was found and how it relates to his situation. Also talk about what needs to happen so the same thing doesn't happen again.

4. Go outside and have impromptu fun together at times! Enjoy!
5. Talk to your child about extra responsibilities as she heads to middle school, about positive behaviors you expect (and have taught), and changes to expect with more students, teachers and classes. Talk about possibly feeling confused but make sure she doesn't pretend to be tough nor get in the wrong crowds to try to fit in. Everybody knows she's new so she doesn't have to impress others.
6. Remember to praise processes, not intelligence, ability, looks or talent. Processes help in a growth mindset, like hard work, sticking to the problem until it's solved, learning from mistakes, and improvements.
7. Sleep is very important to you and your child. Get about 8 hours.
8. Be a sounding board for your child. Ask questions, expect answers with respect and find out more information. Don't jump to conclusions in their drama. They are still children. Listen, think and then act is good for children and parents.
9. Change things up if they are with the same friends all the time and only want to do things with them, especially if just one or two friends. If you haven't before, introduce your child to hobbies and activities with community groups of interest to her for extra support.
10. Know who your children's online friends are and how they interact. Take precautions, be aware as she invites the world into your home.
11. Remember - don't be a friend to your child, be a parent!
12. Some previous research emphasized working with urban boys to support them in discriminatory practices, but new research is noting that the same problems impact girls, too.
13. If she hasn't started an organized notebook for each class yet, 6th grade is a good time to start. See *Elementary Intermediate* chapter for instructions. Use notes to study for tests and change them after each semester. Store all notes in a large binder if preferred. This smaller pocket notebook folder for each class is easier on her back rather than carrying a huge notebook. Oh yeah – organize that locker also!
14. Make sure that she knows how to take class notes. Enroll her in a study skills class if needed. If you can't find one, start one!

15. Make sure he reads increasingly more difficult books, both fiction and nonfiction. Read aloud to each other at times for added connections.
16. Emphasize cooperation and teamwork at home.
17. By now, he should have a hobby based on his creative interests.
18. If you own a small business, talk to her about what you did, do or could have done differently, to be successful. *Entrepreneurial Lit*
19. Try to model relaxation, how to greet others, voice tone, and how to be a friend. This helps you be kinder to each other. You both are under some stress, and this will help both of you and your family.
20. She should know the Multiplication Table by now. Find out about STEM careers and use supplemental math books at home to interest children. [63]
21. Teach your child to write down all assignments in a planner, not relying on memory, and how to organize paperwork, lockers and book bags. Check the planner and the teacher to make sure that papers are turned in on time. Is she journaling? It may help.
22. Teach your child to think critically. This skill is especially needed with a lot information. Learn how to do so yourself, if you need it.
23. If your child is mathematically or verbally gifted, check with the counselor about Talent Search programs and taking the Pre-SAT in 7th grade. This gets her on the college and scholarship path!
24. Teach her how to be courageous and courteous, and do not tolerate bullying by her or her friends. Talk to the guidance counselor at school if there's a problem, and if he doesn't know what to do, that's a red flag area. [64]
25. Figure out solutions, not just consequences, for misbehavior.
26. Help your child manage time wisely. Set a schedule for completing assignments, using a system for study and for recreational reading. Limit screen time to make time for school and home activities.
27. Make sure you help your child grow up since choices made in middle school can lead to high school and after graduation success or problems. He needs to try to think before acting.
28. Talk to your child about opportunities for excelling, being in organizations, being a leader and making the most of middle school.
29. Be consistent and stay involved with your child. Use motivators when needed; use moderation in all things.

30. Teach him how to bounce back or be resilient when bad things happen and how to be proactive by thinking before acting/putting things off.
31. Ask her what she's studying, and give a quick quiz to review it.
32. Expect that your child will continue schooling or training after high school. Begin talking in middle school about the future. Have your child write down his interests and abilities in the journal, begin reading books about others with the same interests and encourage dreaming about plans coming true.
33. Let your children see you sacrifice for the good of the family at times. When you do, they take note.
34. If your child becomes depressed, discouraged or overly negative this will change over time so continue interacting with him. Don't permit too much grumbling-alone time.
35. Continue to talk with your child about sex, drugs and safety! Think: too much adult stuff traps children in situations they cannot handle and the impact can last a lifetime – no matter how mature she thinks she is.
36. When you give children more responsibilities at home during this period, they can earn more trust and freedom.

37. Take time to eat dinner together a few days a week at the table. Talk to each other so you learn more.
38. Make sure that he takes freshmen seminars or support courses that ease the transition into high school. Be aware that more students don't pass ninth grade than any other grade. Plan to make the last year of middle school and first year of high school good years without developing bad habits! If he has bad habits, break them. More students fail 9th grade than all the others.
39. Make sure your children understand non-violence as a way of life by practicing it in your home. Look at the news and your local community to see how it's used and talk with your children about it and attend community meetings on different topics, discuss them. [1]

Why is nonviolence such an important philosophy?
Because it respects the capacity of human beings to grow.
It gives them the opportunity to grow their souls.
And we owe that to each other.
And it took me a long time to realize that. *-Grace Lee Boggs*

High School (9th, 10th, 11th and 12th Grades)

What You Observe

- *High school is different. What changes will happen each year?*
- *There are so many choices! How do we plan and balance them?*
- *How do I help my child make the best decisions?*

Clues for Parents and High School Teens

Every Year in High School: Prepare for the next year and work to be successful! This section is so important that clues for parents and your high school student are offered so that he gets used to taking on more responsibility while heading towards graduation. You still need to review them with him, making sure that he highlights or checks off areas needing discussions or help from you. Take time to do this periodically.

If your child hasn't started a journal yet, this will be a good time for her to begin writing her thoughts, problem solving and making to-do lists as she goes through high school. Writing essays is important in college, so make sure your child writes well. Also, she needs to develop a plan for high school classes she'll take each year in preparation for doing it for college.

Writing in a journal is different from writing in social media which is open to the world. Did you know that some employers look at social media sites before hiring to see what is posted, since that can link to what kind of person your child is? Tell your child to think about the future before posting that negative evidence on line for the world to see! The same can be said about tattoos – sure they're cool, but the message and where its located could also keep jobs from happening in certain fields.

Future planning is important on different levels and we have to be proactive by acting before things happen. To help your child, and possibly yourself, learn about financial literacy to help pay for your future plans. It includes info on managing money, from budgeting, check writing and using credit wisely to saving.

It's also important to be proactive in the sensitive area of sexuality. Talk about abstaining from sex with adolescent girls and boys. When they pledge to do so at a young age and are hopeful and talk about future plans, it sometimes helps in delaying sex. On the other hand, as compared to adolescents and adults in other countries, we lie about sex at times, and use contraceptives less consistently and effectively. That's another contradiction – so talk about contraceptives and safe sex also! Continue to talk with your child about drugs, respecting their bodies and safety. Think: too much adult stuff traps children in situations they cannot handle and the impact can last a lifetime – no matter how mature she thinks she is or you try to hide from it.

Keep the following in mind as your child begins high school. Your children need to become proficient in school work and ready for college and/or an entry-level job. If proficient, students shouldn't have to take remedial or developmental classes when they enter college. These classes are really high school classes that you pay for, they do not count towards the major and they keep students in college longer. The Common Core is online all across the country so use it to help your child help himself. There are no secrets to being proficient.

Also, do what you, as a parent, need to do for your future and don't let pride, your peers nor family keep you from training beyond high school if your plans didn't work out earlier in life. Whether it's a GED. college or vocational school or a certificate in something you can do it! Read different perspectives on training after high school. [65]

Times have changed. As you noticed, it's not as easy to plan for life after graduation since there are so many choices and it can cost so much. You and your child have to plan early and keep working at it. College costs too much to play your way through it now and the stakes are higher with harder to find jobs! Check with your counselor about taking college courses for free, possibly. With good grades, a positive attitude, leadership, community service, career research and financing, your child's future dreams can and will come true!

Students need to understand that high school is like checkers and college is like chess. They have different rules and players.

9th Grade (Freshman Year) Clues for Parents

The ninth grade, as the first year in high school, is a year of changes or transitions and is the most important year for high school success. More students fail ninth grade than any other year. The cognitive, emotional and physical parts of adolescence have kicked in, and your children are learning about many things not in the books or classes. They are no longer the oldest students in school, they are now the youngest. They have to maneuver a much larger school facility with more new students from all over the city with new responsibilities, possibilities and temptations.

Balance is needed since this is the middle to high school transition for your parenting skills. Balance letting your child go in small steps so she makes choices and tastes a little freedom with responsibility, *but* keep your eyes and ears open. Students have new homework pressures and anxieties in high school so parents still have to make sure that no bad habits start or are carried on from middle school. Be nosy if needed so you know what's going on. Let him know you'll back off some as you see him taking on and successfully handling more responsibilities. By now you view the news together at times, use this as discussion starters about life in general.

You want your child to have fun at times, but not all the time. It's best to participate in supervised after-school activities, since those are risky hours when juvenile crimes and adult-like stuff are most likely to happen. Running with an older crowd is not good for your teen nor for your peace of mind. Teach your child to think about consequences to decisions before acting by listing the possible pros and cons of activities she's considering.

Parents have a tendency to visit schools less as children get older, but they should visit even more. Continue going to meetings and open houses, stay in contact with teachers and keep on top of your child's grades and other activities. As parents, don't get too involved in the drama that students may participate in. Check this guide book every year as your teen transitions to the next grade and look for clues to what's really going on.

Freshman year starts the permanent grade record (GPA = grade point average) that will follow her after graduation on the transcript and entry job resume. GPA can determine eligibility for college or vocational training. Learning new organization skills is necessary so your teen has a balanced life, with time for school work, family, friends and activities. Working for money to buy things should be a summer activity so his job is being a good student during the year. Parents may want to organize also.

Make sure your adolescents have positive ideas as action oriented leaders, not just followers waiting for things to happen. They need to persevere or keep trying to get the results that they want. They need to learn quickly and use their brains and feelings to solve problems. They need to learn more about themselves and be committed to being their BEST self as they plan their futures. This idea and those that follow, with your commitment as parents and families, will get your adolescents on the right track. [66]

Clues for First Year Students

Congratulations! You are in the first generation of students who will complete all twelve years of school in the 21st century! Check off or circle important areas you need to work on as you make this year the start of your high school success. Discuss the earlier *Parent Clues* with them.

1. Remember that it's okay to "say no" to potentially bad situations and to blame your mother for not going along with the crowd! Always think safety and possible consequences for your actions. Don't follow your friends and their actions if you know that they're wrong! Think for yourself and think about your life! Unfortunately, too many friends regret not making decisions that included safety.

2. Learn to organize information, support your arguments and express yourself clearly as needed for literacy now and in college.

3. Don't put off school work - do it as soon as you have the time, using good time management. Work before and after practice or activities plus make time for 7 hours sleep by going to bed earlier. You've seen your sleep-crazed friends in action! Don't join them!

4. Be aware that most colleges require four years of English, three years of social studies, math, science and two years foreign language, and physical education. Think about taking advantage of college classes while they are free if you have the grades and the time! Schedule extracurricular activities with assignments that are due in your planner.

5. By now you should know math facts, laws and rules and the multiplication table [67] and not rely on calculators all the time. This will build confidence and you'll do better in math. Try it!

6. Making friends may be tough, but when you participate in activities after school (extracurricular), you may meet others with similar interests who may become your friends.

7. Become a leader. It looks good on your resume, it will help you get scholarships along with community service and it's good for you!

8. Don't force yourself to be "cool" to be popular. It may get in the way of your studies…and get on your parents' nerves! Be patient and positive to make good friends, don't get stuck with friend/enemies!

9. It can be overwhelming to be the youngest students in a large high school. So, note the time it takes to move from class to class and don't linger. Don't show off insecure behaviors because you're nervous. Learn to be confident with positive attitudes about new things learned.

10. Consider advanced or AP courses if you qualify. They help in college.

11. By now, you know that it's not your smarts, looks, talent or abilities that help you succeed. It's the processes you go through that are most important, like your hard work, sticking to the problem until solved, learning from mistakes, etc. Give yourself these pep talks now!
12. Approach your studies as preparation for your future dream job.
13. If you are bored, do something more challenging. (Bored people are sometimes boring!) Read good books! A world of interests await you – if you reach out. If you can't think of anything else, check out all the web sites in this guide to learn more about you and your future.
14. If your friends/peer group put you down for studying, organize a study group and invite them to join you. If not, don't let haters bother you.
15. Get help from a tutor, go online or use introductory books to learn new information (make sure it matches the topics you need), and talk with the school or community librarian when needed. Get help if your skills are not where they need to be. You're old enough to get it done!
16. **16.** Be serious: Plan your future and stick to your plans! You must have at the least one full year or more of training or college after graduation to be successful in the future, but graduating college is even better! Take an interest inventory to figure out what your interests are. See your guidance counselor and on-line sites. [68] Take them more than once.
17. Stay engaged in learning and involved in volunteering or service learning. Your "job" is to do your best in school now for the future.
18. If you're athletic or participate in other activities taking a lot of time, remember that being a good student comes first (student-athletes). Athletes, models and other roles that rely on the body should always have a back-up plan. It will come in handy in case something unexpected happens that keeps your body inactive. You don't have control over everything so be proactive!

10th Grade (Sophomore Year) Clues for Parents

Your sophomore needs more freedom, but within structure and boundaries. You should have established consequences for misbehavior (going to a gadget-filled room is not a good consequence) and enforce them, giving rewards when earned. [70] Even if your teen did well in ninth grade, she can't slowdown in the tenth. Whether she has homework or not, she should review the information covered the previous day in classes. If she's not buckling down, ask her what she has written in her notebook for each class (and she should be writing notes daily) and what was covered in the textbook daily. This helps prepare them for college or training after graduation.

Teens like to make their own choices, when practical, rather than you choosing everything for him. They may rebel when forced, so follow this process at times. To make his own choices, he needs to write down answers to the following questions: Put the problem at the top of the page. Brainstorm a list of pros and cons. Which seems to be more important? What are possible consequences of each point? Which go along with your plans? What's the wiser and smarter choice? What will you do? What would your parents prefer, and why?

Sophomore Clues for Students

After discussing Parent Clues with your parents, reread the Freshman Clues to determine if you followed each tip. Highlight or circle areas that you need to backtrack on and use your journal to begin lists to improve!

1. This is a good year to seriously learn how to plan for being away from home. Start doing your own laundry; cook, not just warm up family meals at times; wash your own clothes; set and live within a budget, etc.
2. High school is filled with both joy and stress. You may have to balance school work and community service, dating, sports and other activities. If your parents can support you, it's best to spend time being a good student rather than working during the school year. Learn to manage your time. Know when and how to ask for help, and learn when to say no. Don't follow the crowd if it's wrong.
3. You should be on a technical career or college path by now and have a plan as you think seriously about the future. Learn more about jobs of the future, including tech careers with certification. [71]
4. If you are good in math and science and you have what it takes to persevere, think about engineering as a possible major in college. [72] Find a college with co-op programs so you can work 4-7 months per year making money, gaining experience with a company while taking college courses. Later, analytical skills will be useful in any career.
5. Take a foreign language that you might need in your career. College grads with foreign language skills can get better jobs. [73]
6. When assigned long-term projects, use parts of the *SMART FAMILY* plan to get started. Begin working soon after they are assigned so you don't forget critical points. Make a schedule to complete your work in a timely manner, and submit it. Learn from your teachers' responses.
7. Determine electives based on your interests or college future, not just because the subject seems easy or your friends like that elective.
8. You need to take math every year so do a good job in your studies.

9. Select two or three things that you do well and you're passionate about for extracurricular activities and/or work on a hobby. Become well-rounded because it will come in handy when you're on your own.

10. By now, your note taking skills should be important to your learning, especially when you go to college or into a technical field. You can't keep all that info in your head.

11th Grade (Junior Year) Clues for Parents

Keep communication lines open. If your child needs to pay more attention to his grades, help him learn better time management and study skills. Ask counselors for help if he needs extra support or tell him to do it but to bring you proof. Continue to talk about future plans and staying on track, especially if her plans are her own. If she has been serious in high school, make sure that she avoids burnout. If she hasn't been serious, the reality of junior year should be a wake-up call.

Your child may get that first part-time job and a driver's license this year. Think about your limits and his maturity. There is a fine line between being overly protective and being cautious. Students need to continue learning responsibility, and you need to continue giving consequences. Too many future plans can be hurt by one thoughtless act.

By now you should have taught your children both interdependence (where he learns to depend on others) and independence (where he learns to work alone at times). Don't hover as they go to college or training after high school! Research has shown that hovering parents can possibly create adolescents who may not grow up until their 30's -- though some children don't grow up on their own! Teach them well throughout their lives so they learn to rely on their own capabilities as they mature, and expect them to grow up! Check out the *Special Section for Parents* in *Chapter 13* for clues to possibly use for youth trying to be grown.

Clues for Junior Students After discussing earlier Parent Clues with parents, reread the Sophomore Clues to determine if you followed each tip. If not, begin lists in your journal for improvement! It's time to get serious!

1. By now study skills should be a breeze! Begin accelerating study routines, club leadership, volunteering and learn more about certificate programs or college majors and careers.

2. Strive to make wiser choices and decisions,

3. Explore your talents and prepare emotionally for life after graduation. Grow up, but not too fast! Don't let poor choices mess up your future so think about consequences!

4. Locate the *Occupational Outlook Handbook* online or at the library to learn about different occupations, trends and majors. Search for programs or courses that interest you. This is your life you're planning!
5. This can be a rigorous year to raise the Grade Point Average (GPA) for your transcript. Do not take easier courses to get a higher GPA. It can backfire. Remember that what you learn now will help in college.

A lot is going on, but don't get stressed. If your GPA is too low for certain colleges or training programs, you may need to revise your plans. It's okay, be honest with yourself and be positive. You will be successful if you put enough effort and positive energy into your plans. Plus, it's always wise to have more than one plan in case you need to change them.

12th Grade (Senior Year) Clues for Parents
You made it to the last year, but don't celebrate yet! The last year of high school can be stressful for you as you decide if your child is ready for the future. Plus, there are many deadlines to meet. Make sure your near-graduate is ready for life after home by doing her own laundry, as she cooks nutritious meals, budgets, uses alarms and takes more responsibility.

As your child plans on leaving home, you may begin to get the empty-nest syndrome. It's normal. This may coincide with major life changes such as menopause, retirement, or taking care of elderly parents. Talk to others who have gone through the same thing. Plan on helping yourself adjust to this new change. Make a checklist of things that you will need for the graduation process.

Clues for Senior Students After discussing earlier *Parent Clues*, reread the *Junior Clues* to determine if you followed each tip. If not, get your journal out, again, to begin improvement lists. Your future is happening sooner rather than later.

1. Avoid senioritis since you haven't graduated yet!
2. Plan for college, training or work and take an interest inventory if you haven't yet. Have you thought about your interests, abilities, experiences, and what you're passionate about? This will help you determine which path you'll take after graduation. Look at your journal – have you written things that give you hints of that new path?

3. Make sure that your grades don't slip this last year because some colleges and training businesses will check your senior grades. Take a full schedule during this last year, even if you finished your credits. Your GPA will follow you until you land that first job.
4. Look seriously at how much your friends, family members, and you – drink alcohol and/or take pills. If people in your family have addictions, resolve to break the cycle. It's hard on your family even if you think that being high helps you. Think about the financial and personal costs of substance use and think moderation in all things!
5. Consider taking free college courses this last year if you've fulfilled all your credits and time was limited earlier - if your grades are good enough. Check out the technical, other info in *Sophomore Clues.*
6. This last year of high school is important to your future life: make wise choices and decisions that are good for life and your future!
7. Have fun but stay balanced with study, safety and future preparations.

If you don't stand up for something, you'll fall for anything.
–Malcolm X

Education is that whole system of human training
within and without the school house walls,
which molds and develops men [and women]. *– W.E.B. DuBois*

<<<<<<<<<<<<<<<<<<<<>>>>>>>>>>>>>>>>>>>>
Are you where you want to be at this stage?
Take the summer to get yourself together for your future!!!!
<<<<<<<<<<<<<<<<<<<<>>>>>>>>>>>>>>>>>>>>

Lord, Grant me the Serenity
to accept the things I cannot change,
Courage to change the things I can,
And wisdom to know the difference. …

Dios, concédeme la serenidad
para aceptar las cosas que no puedo cambiar,
Valor para cambiar aquellas que puedo,
y sabiduría para reconocer la diferencia. [74]
--Reinhold Niebuh

Twenty-seven Serious College Preps for Students

College is like chess and high school is like checkers, from preparing to go there, to differing sets of responsibilities, to the coursework, to handling assignments and discussions, to other decisions you make. Don't make the mistake of handling college like high school since you will not be successful if you do. Even if you are not going to college, some of the following plans may be useful steps for you as you prepare for some type of training or certificate program. Make sure you pay attention to the following points as you prepare for college or for training after graduation.

Ninth Grade

1. Check your family college savings Plan 529. View the Federal Student Aid website to research career and college options and prerequisites.
2. Be aware that most colleges require English, three years of social studies, math, science and two-three years of foreign language, physical education, and other electives.
3. Take honors and advanced courses if your grades even border on being good enough. They help you prepare for college and scholarships!
4. Take advantage of college classes while they are free if you have the grades! Join a study or college prep group and learn collaboration.
5. Develop a plan for college choices since in-state is cheaper than out of state. It takes money to go to college so let your brain power get you a scholarship. You need grades, leadership and community service to set your application apart.
6. If you work, begin saving, but that's chump change compared to the Ivy League scholarship that your brain power and income level can possibly get for you. Think about it and apply in 11th grade. [75]
7. Be aware that essays are important in college exams, so make sure you have good writing skills. How well you do on placement exams, not just your interests, sometimes determine courses you can take in college so be serious.

Tenth Grade

8. Meet with your counselor and find a mentor to discuss college requirements and check websites. Don't let your future fall to chance! Imagine it and plan – you can always change your plans, but start one!
9. Work on a list of colleges or training programs to apply to.

10. Take pre-assessments like the PSAT or PLAN to get comfortable with the format and types of questions.

11. Begin visiting college campuses over the summer.

Eleventh Grade: Almost there!

12. Fall Semester: You must take the Preliminary SAT/National Merit Scholarship Qualifying Test (PSAT/NMSQT) if your grades are high enough to see if you qualify for scholarships and programs.

13. Spring Semester: Register and take SAT or ACT for college admission. Take the test more than once since colleges take the highest scores. Pay application fees or get a waiver from your counselor if you qualify.

14. Understand different types of financial aid and payment options for college. College is expensive so have alternate plans for community college, then transfer to a 4 year school if needed. Or earn a certificate and go to work while attending college on-line part-time. Some businesses pay for college. Do your research!

15. Investigate scholarships to see if you meet the requirements. It's a lot of work but your future life will be easier if you get it! You only know if you try! Try Ivy League colleges if you can meet the prerequisites.

16. Take AP & rigorous classes, working to become better every year!

17. Continue on your selected path and don't let too much fun and being on the edge stop your dreams. Take care of business so you can work on your goals – you know what I mean!

18. Talk to students in families like yours whose children went to college.

19. Don't stress, even though you have a lot to do. If your GPA is too low for certain colleges, then apply to other ones.

20. Juniors are expected to take a challenging math course this year since you will take math the first year of college, no matter what major. Know how and when to use math tools and know math laws and rules.

21. Summer Before 12th Grade: Narrow down your college choices. Apply for waivers if needed. Complete your applications. Make sure you check prerequisites to see if you meet them. If not, revise again!

22. Begin thinking about your college major. [76]

12th Grade:: Don't relax yet – you still have deadlines to meet!

23. Fall: Develop a calendar to schedule test dates, due dates, deadlines, recommendations, and transcripts. Conduct a scholarship search. Attend financial aid workshops.

24. Winter: Don't procrastinate or put off what you need to do.
    a. Pay attention and schedule due dates for applications and apply for waivers with your counselor to see if you can.
    b. Make copies of everything before sending to colleges.
    c. Contact colleges to make sure they received your applications.
    d. Apply early for financial aid: first come, first served.
    e. Estimate your taxes, don't wait until April. Submit the FAFSA (financial aid form) right after January 1st.

25. Spring: You will get your acceptance letters and financial aid offers by mid-April. Visit your final college choice before accepting the offer. Make your final choice by May 1.

26. Summer: Ask your high school to send final transcripts to selected colleges. Notify colleges you won't attend. Look at your budget, then begin buying things for your college room if you haven't started yet. Plan and stay safe during the summer! Partying too hard may derail your plans!

27. Make plans to transition into college so you stay there– and try to stay in college til graduation.

By now you should have seen your counselor. You need transcripts, possible signatures, etc. If needed, ask your parents to call the counselor or the principal if you haven't scheduled an appointment. Keep going back or persevere!.

As you make the final preparations for college or training beyond high school, the following points may be useful. Refer to the Occupational Outlook Handbook so you learn more about your potential major or career. Learn about your career interests [77]. Be serious as you plan for training or college and develop a plan for finishing your training program or graduate in 4 years to keep expenses down. Decide on a major in your area of interest. Do not switch majors many times since that adds to your semesters in college. Many people get jobs in areas that are similar, not exactly linked to their majors or training so you don't need to be exact.

Shoot for the moon. Even if you miss it,
you will land among the stars.

--Les Brown

12. Adult Choices after Graduation

But the person who scored well on an SAT will not necessarily be the best doctor or the best lawyer or the best businessman. These tests do not measure character, leadership, creativity, perseverance.

--William Julius Wilson

What You Observe

- *Your child graduated, and needs training after high school, but money is tight so she will attend college later.*
- *Your adult child has returned home to live with you.*
- *You are underemployed, out of work or need to try something new.*

Living in the 2010s and beyond demands continuous learning, feeling positive, thinking critically and planning for the unexpected. It's past time to be serious. Your child needs to understand that college or training are necessary after high school graduation for future success.

You may be underemployed or out of work and thinking about reading this chapter for yourself. You are not alone since many adults of all ages are returning to school (whether adult education, community or 4 year college or some kind of training), going to school for the first time, retooling their skills in a new training program or attending counseling sessions for personal issues. This sends a powerful message to your children that you are taking care of business, possibly spurring them to want to do something positive and different also. Changing old habits is good!

The real test is life: who you and your children have grown to be!

A Special Section for Parents with ...

a) Grads Not Considering College or Training
b) Former Students Who Dropped-Out of High School
c) Adult Children Who May Return Home

1. As parents, think about your independent lifestyle without grown children and how you live now or you're planning to live. Make sure that you protect your time, your place and your space, if possible. You love them, but adult children are now really guests in your home, and you want your home to be a peaceful multi-generational home.

2. Be upfront with what you expect of your adult child. She needs responsibilities with consequences so you are not raising them again. Discuss this before moving in, right after high school ends or right after she drops out of school. This may help her decide to grow up quicker and leave home.
3. You want him to act like an adult with responsibilities, so have a family meeting soon after arrival home (or preferably before returning) to create lists of all household responsibilities. Divide the list with expectations that everyone carries their fair share with rules and penalties for not following the rules.
4. Make sure your adult child keeps a journal and develops action plans for gaining skills and breaking old patterns, if needed, so she can leave home (possibly again). She may have to review and use the chapter on *Preparing for Change or Renewal.* Then work through the *Jobs after High School* list with the OOH. [78]
5. If chapters in this book don't have the information they seek, then your adult child should use your preferred browser to find articles that relate to why he hasn't left home, what his issues are and how he needs to solve his problems so he can run his life. The goal will be a list of issues that have to be discussed and written about in the journal for preparing to leave – again if needed.
6. If your adult child has children (your grandchildren or your great-grandchildren) she's bringing into your home, she needs to understand that they are not your children. She has to raise them with this Guidebook and they also have to conform to house rules.
7. Your adult child may also need to review and discuss critical thinking and decision making sections of this Guide.
8. Set rules for adult sleepovers, possibly requiring adult child celibacy. t
9. A part time legitimate job, at the least, should be required to help with rent and/or household expenses, not just their own expenses. Money needs to be saved for leaving the family home.
10. Set a time frame for leaving with your guests and stick with it or renegotiate if needed. Don't ignore it. [79]
11. If your adult child does not want to help with expenses, house rules or household chores, then it may be best that your adult child and you make the decision for your adult child to not return to your home. It's your house and your time that you've earned, and you don't want to be held hostage by out of control adult children!
12. Make sure you protect your identity, legal needs and have a will.[41]

What You Need to Do for Your Graduate or Yourself

Your time is limited, so don't waste it living someone else's life. Don't let the noise of others' opinions drown out your inner voice and most important, have the courage to follow your heart and intuition. – *Steve Jobs*

1. Hopefully: you began saving for college expenses early in your child's life, you have a savings account to fall back on or saved in your state's College Savings Plan 529; and/or your child can qualify fo scholarships and internships. Talk to others about what they did.
2. Look at where YOU are now… Did you fulfill YOUR dreams from the past, or did "life" change your plans? Are your skills marketable today? Do you have skills but you are unsure of what they really are? Take some career quizzes online or check your local Adult Education.
3. Need help in going back to finish that GED or college degree? Check out Adult Education and other initiatives in your state. Will your job pay you to go back? Ask them – you never know until you do so.
4. If your reading and writing skills are a little rusty, call the Adult Education Office in your county and do the work to build literacy.
5. If you are a veteran, contact your State Higher Education Agency to find money to pay for college.
6. Check with jobs or community organizations where you participate. They may have scholarships that your child can qualify for because of your membership. You never know if you don't ask!
7. Reinvent your skills. Gain the skills you need to move beyond where you are right now as you become the change you desire. You can do it!
8. Clues to use when you get a job: report to work on time; follow work rules; practice good listening; ask questions; dress appropriately; have a positive attitude; be respectful and be flexible.
9. Clues to keep a job include: understand your boss' expectations and your role; keep personal emotions away from work; don't gossip; show initiative; show respect to your boss at all times; accept change; learn your weak areas and improve your skills; develop positive relationships; keep work info separate from social media and continuously learn.

Remember that some jobs are limited during this period. Inexperienced and new workers are competing for the same jobs as experienced and educated workers from around the world at times. Put your best foot forward as you learn new skills. If you are serious about change, help is available: check out local and state initiatives for going back to school and use their information as you continue to learn.

Beware of scams. Unscrupulous people are out there who want to get your private information to take your hard earned money and to harm your credit. Read and really hear what's being written and said, especially online where information is exchanged quickly. Check to make sure it is a legitimate business and use online reviews to learn what other people said about them before giving out your information. Learn to protect yourself and your family. [80]

The following section offers general information that may differ regionally or even in the same state. In other words, how one group runs its program may differ from others with the same name. Find out all you can before giving out too much personal information.

Education after High School Can Include:

1. **On-the-Job Training** – apply to work for a business that will train you as you work.
2. **Co-Op Education** –a type of internship program for college students with paid career training as you work and take college courses.
3. **Apprentices** – complete a 3-4 year training program that combines on-the-job training with technical and educational instruction.
4. **Private Business or Trade School** – short term training (1 month – 1 year) for jobs such as cosmetology or truck driving. Costs vary from trade school to trade school.
5. **Check trends** and locations in industries that are hiring in areas like mechanical engineering and technology. Use the Occupational Outlook Handbook to find trends, then get the training.
6. **Community College** – one semester to two year school offering vocational and technical programs leading to certificates, diplomas or associate degrees. They also offer remedial courses. Do well in high school so you don't have to pay to repeat high school courses!
7. **College or University** –a four year minimum program with entrance requirements based on high school grades and college entrance test scores. Students may apply for application waivers– talk to your

counselor. Scholarships and grants are possible if you are a good student and you take the time to complete applications. Only four US colleges do not charge traditional tuition since students work on campus to earn it. Check them out - one may be located near you!

8. **Some jobs** pay for its workers to go to college.
9. **Military** – work for the USA; get training, pay, room and board and benefits. For high school or GED grads only.
10. Programs like the **Job Corps -** a free education and training program that helps low-income young people (at least 16 years old) learn a career, earn a high school diploma or GED, then find and keep a good job. Your child may need this.
11. **Volunteering** with low pay, but satisfaction with work experiences occurs in these three settings:

    Peace Corps for college grads or exchange program.

    AmeriCorps Volunteers in Service to America /VISTA –an antipoverty program for 17 - 24 year old students who are in college.

    Student Conservation Associates with jobs and internships for college students who are18 or older.
12. Check out **infrastructure jobs**: for building and maintaining water pipes, power grids, transit lines with on-the-job training.
13. Another option: sustainable **agriculture** or agricultural business, including urban farming if you have space
14. Look at your interests and abilities to get a **job** or to become an **entrepreneur or small business owner -** if you have know-how and passion about a hobby or skills and have financing. See the Small Business Administration (SBA) at your library.
15. Experience another culture by **living abroad** with a host family if you know another language and have the funds.
16. **Internships** are programs that provide practical experience for beginners in an occupation or profession. Some of them give stipends.

Teach your students to use what talents they have;
the woods would be silent if no bird sang
except those who sing best. *--Anonymous*

Whew! We've come this far by faith!

PART IV

Our Schools Are Up to Us, Too!

We can, whenever and wherever we choose,
successfully teach all children whose schooling is of interest…
We already know more than we need to do that.
Whether or not we do it must finally depend on
how we feel about the fact that we haven't so far.
--Ron Edmonds, 1978

As a next step in your development as parents of students in the 21st century, you may find that your attention is needed in another important area. You may have worked with your children as their BEST teacher at home, and are pleased with your results. You want that to continue into formal schooling with learning and fair treatment that prepares your children for their futures.

You want the schools your children attend to be good matches for you and your children. If they are not good matches and the assigned school has observable problems, you don't have to accept the way thing are. You may have to pull out your parent voice and advocate for school changes.

Public schools belong to the public,
not just to parents who send their children there.

Schools are a public responsibility and everyone has the right to advocate for them and criticize them. When schools need improvement, or when they don't, parent advocates are needed to make sure student needs are being met and students are being prepared for their futures.

This last part of the book offers additional information and resources so school stakeholders can become effective partners with schools while advocating for improvements.

We must view young people not as empty bottles to be filled,
but as candles to be lit. *–Robert H. Shaffer*

13. Family Options in Selecting Schools

Quality schools have excellent instructional programs, especially in reading and mathematics. They have a school culture that values students and listens to them. They personalize learning and have strong connections to parents and their communities. As parents, you always need to be aware of what's going on with your children in schools, whether they attend schools considered as quality or not. Some of the advocacy skills and resources in this last part of the guide may help with issues you or your children may encounter.

When you select schools, think about the needs of your child and family. Don't select a school based on tradition or what they used to do since the school may have gone through changes in personnel and policies. See if the school is a good fit by finding school brochures that describe it either online or at the district offices. Look at the school curricula, learning philosophy; academic performance; disciplinary policies; before- and after-school activities; safety policies; reputation; parent and community involvement; facilities, services and admissions processes. [81]

Visit schools to see how they are run. When you visit, pay attention to what you see, hear, smell and how you feel about the interactions you see in the school. This will give you information about the school culture and climate, which explains the quality of school life and some of its rules, traditions, beliefs and policies. Compare what you see and sense with the brochure. If you have questions about anything, write them down.

Policies are school rules that explain how the school is organized. Ask to see the policies, but note that not all policies are written. Make an appointment with the principal to learn more about what you saw. Ask questions about any differences you noticed in the written policies and explanations and school brochure. Ask questions about the school's reputation that may be talked about in the community. Remember to take the list of questions with you and of course, be courteous so you make a good first impression.

Some families attend the public schools in their neighborhood that are assigned to them. You are fortunate if your assigned school is a good match for your child and family. If the assigned public school is not a good match based on state assessment or test scores, or if is unsafe, you still may have a few options or choices under the Elementary and Secondary Education Act. This act offers equal access to education, high standards and accountability. Enacted in 1965, the Act emphasizes education reform priorities and it is reissued every decade or so. Recent updates have included No Child Left Behind (NCLB), the American Recovery and Reinvestment Act and the new

Every Child Achieves Act (ECAA).

Keep up to date on the Every Child Achieves Act [82] so you are aware of any differences from what's initially and briefly reported in this guide.

If your assigned school was designated as needing improvement, various things could have happened to it. Some low-performing schools were closed or restarted under direction of a charter (if your state decides to offer charter schools) or education management organization. Schools may be restructured as turnaround schools with replacement of half the staff. Another model is that of transformation schools where teachers are held accountable for student growth. These models may change over time.

Your child could receive supplemental educational services (free tutoring) if available in your district. The district is required to give parents a list of organizations that offer this tutoring. Another form of extra assistance is the school's Response to Intervention (RTI) services which is discussed in the next chapter.

Other families have more options. They may live in districts with good public schools, they can pay to transfer their children to better schools in other districts, or send them to private or religious schools. They can attend magnet programs that are sometimes run like private schools within public schools for desegregation purposes. This seems inequitable unless the magnet philosophy is offered to the whole school so all students receive those services, too.

Some families may choose virtual or internet schools though they can isolate children unless parents or the school schedules real time for socialization with other children. They may choose public charter schools run by private companies if their state allows them to operate. Home schooling is another option when parents know what to do and make the time to plan and schedule lessons at home. Most options are limited since space for all students is limited, even if parents can afford them. Hopefully all schools strive to become quality schools for the good of all their students.

Learn from yesterday,
live for today,
hope for tomorrow.

--Albert Einstein

14. Speak Up to Find Solutions

Some people learn from their mistakes, others avoid making many mistakes by learning from the mistakes of others. *--Kahlil Gilbran*

Staying engaged in your children's elementary, middle and high schools is a necessary part of their education. It looks different at each level, but it is necessary. When parents are not involved, children may slack off too. Your involvement also sends a clearer message that you expect your child to achieve, and you expect that teachers, when their teaching is reinforced at home, will help them to succeed, too. Let your child know that you and the teacher are partners who want school to be a good experience. You also want your child to learn what she can do in a nice way to help the teacher teach her.

Your child's behavior may change at the beginning of the year, and he may complain about social issues, like his teacher doesn't like him, or plays favorites, or he's bored, or we all get punished if someone does something bad. Sometimes the actions of your children demand that you shift your actions to find solutions to problems which may make you uncomfortable. The following clues may help you continue linking home with school even when you may be under stress.

When the teacher contacts you or you need to contact the teacher

1. Don't panic if this is your first time in this experience.
   a. Ask questions so you and the teacher are on the same page and can create a plan to help your child. Be nice!
   b. Ask for specifics so you can judge the help your child or the teacher needs, write questions down and take notes on what's said.
   - Some questions to ask: is it every class or just one? Is the work not being done or is he frustrated and can't handle it? Is it a recurring problem? How was the situation handled?
   - Try not to place blame yet since the focus is on working together for the good of your child. Try to reassure the teacher so he doesn't feel criticized. Keep calm and repeat that you're trying to understand what's going on.

- Ask if a meeting needs to be scheduled to talk about a problem you don't understand, hoping that with her help you can solve it.
- Ask other questions to find out what is going on and how you can help. Take notes to share with your child's other parent and with your child.
- Brainstorm solutions with the teacher.
- Expect that your child will follow through on clues for school and home so the issue is resolved and hopefully won't happen again. If it does, calmly repeat needed parts of the process.

c. Follow up with the teacher a few weeks later to see if the situation has improved. Get additional help from the school counselor.

2. Talk to your child when the teacher brings something up that needs to be cleared up or your child mentions discontent that you need to learn more about. Work together so your child won't get away with misconceptions or assume that you don't care.

   a. Don't take what she says as "truth" which could be a grey area.

   b. Take notes on what your child says and use that when you talk to the teacher. Ask questions: what did the teacher say exactly? What was happening in class at the time? What did you do? What was everybody else doing?

   c. If he says the teacher was "mean," it could be that the teacher makes him do his work. After you meet with the teacher, you'll know more about whether she has a grumpy personality. If so, explain that the teacher is trying to teach him the behaviors needed in her class and your child shouldn't take it personally.

   d. Find out why your child feels a certain way, not that you will fix the problem that the teacher has. You want your child to learn tools to help herself, like talking to the teacher after class to explain to her what you feel, since she may not know that.

3. Write notes down and any questions you have before going to school.

4. If you need to, <u>volunteer</u> to help in the class a few days so you can observe interactions between the teacher, your child and other students. Use this info to also explain why your child shouldn't take things personal.

5. If you find that the teacher is not doing much to help in the situation, you have choices:

   a. Tell your child that she has to get used to that person while learning to work with different types of personalities.

b. Advocate for your child if you feel that's the best way to handle the situation and you feel the teacher is especially hard on him. At this level talk with adults to find out more information. You can talk to the guidance counselor or youth service center coordinator for how other parents may have handled situations similar to yours. Ask the principal for advice on what to do. If things stay the same, try to change classrooms.

c. After investigating issues and you happen to find that the same thing occurs again with other families, the school may be a big part of the problem. If you go to another school and find some of the same things happen again, maybe you need to work through some of the above clues again. Or maybe you need to work on yourself if you have a bad habit of reacting the same way.

Additional Information.

1. If your child needs additional support in math and other subjects, ask about your school's Response to Intervention (RTI) services. Ask: Is there a school wide community of support? A support class during the school day? After school tutoring? Extended class time? Summer instruction? What else do they offer? Note: allowing low-achieving students to take remedial courses is not a recipe for academic success.
2. Be supportive. If you like the teacher and school, tell her principal and other parents.
3. Always attend parent conferences and contact teachers sooner rather than later.
4. Even if you're upset, don't complain about or criticize the teacher in front of your child. It undermines the authority of the teacher and your children will follow your lead. Keep your feelings to yourself or other adults, the administration and the teacher.
5. Follow through on what you say you're going to do about discipline problems, and don't make a promise to the teacher if you're not. Even if your child makes a mistake, there should be consequences, so take the time to discipline your child in a timely manner.
6. Don't make excuses for your child or the teacher. It's okay to apologize early on, but help the school hold your child accountable and you hold teachers accountable if mistakes occur. Don't bail your child out by making excuses. Teach life lessons that could prevent her from making bigger mistakes in the future.

7. If bullying is a problem, stop it early in its tracks. This should occur if your child is a bully or if your child is being bullied. Reach out for help if needed with the counselor or youth service center.
8. ***Homework.*** During homework your child is struggling and you try to help, but your child says, "But my teacher didn't do it that way!"
   a. Ask your child if the teacher says that students can get the answer in different ways, which is usually yes. Get your answer, then tell your child to explain to you what she could have done to get the same answer. And you can explain yours. Sometimes she just doesn't want your help. Back off if you have to. If she feels okay later, she may ask for help.
   b. You know your strengths, so before problems happen, find a library book that explains different ways to do problems for that grade. (Buy that book, used, online for a few pennies and postage). Ask them if they see the preferred way. Maybe then it will be easier for them to accept parental help.
   c. Or write your answer out and leave it on the desk so he can see your method the next day. Then talk calmly about different ways of finding answers. Use their content standards to support your work if needed.
   d. Never do your children's homework. They will not learn that way, and a good teacher can tell the difference!

When teachers and school personnel go the extra mile (really where they need to be) and show they care, parents need to let them know they're appreciated periodically!

Saying thank you can be difficult…
I need the help of others to survive…
the human race is interdependent.
We cannot live life alone.
We …constantly rely on each other for all kinds of resources…
When I say thank you I am acknowledging …
something from another human being.

--Family Friend Poems.com

It takes 7 P's for success: Patience, pride, passion, perseverance, partners, performance and play! **--***Will Allen, Growing Food/Justice forAll*

15. School Influencers

School influencers have the capacity or power to impact decisions made about how schools are run. Schools are influenced by national conditions and people in schools with power. Our nation has practiced deep patterns of exclusion where some people are denied good things that others receive. These patterns affect our schools through discriminatory educational policies, economic practices, rules and laws.

Laws influence how schools are run, but it's the individual states, school systems and schools that impact the day to day operations of schools through another level of policies, school funding and rules. Events in schools are influenced locally by the actions of people – from teachers who teach to parents who send their children to school as students. The classroom interactions between teachers and students are key to whether students learn or not. It's what all school stakeholders do that makes a difference in student achievement. All school stakeholders are connected to student achievement - no one group does this alone. Thus, all stakeholders need to learn new skills to better support teaching and learning in classrooms.

Since classroom interactions are fast-paced and sometimes stress-filled, some teachers may not have time to think about their responses to classroom situations – they just react. That's why they need to be familiar with any personal tendencies toward prejudged opinions since the results of quick actions may intentionally or unintentionally exclude some children and treat them unfairly. Educators also need to acknowledge and learn from how they were taught when they were young since these behaviors can also surface in fast-paced situations.

Stereotypical images … are powerful in influencing
what people see and expect….
Unless educators consciously … work against … stereotypes,
they often act … unconsciously.
Our assumptions … are so deeply entrenched…
it is virtually impossible for us
not to hold them
unless we take conscious … deliberate action.

---Pedro Noguera

These situations can show up when teachers are under stress with students. It's like parents who later realize they reacted to stressful situations with their children as their parents did with them, even though they said they would never do that! You know the feeling.

To keep unconscious choices down, educators need the competencies and the confidence to reach and teach all their students. They need to critically think about what they're doing and feeling – and both teachers and their students need to be engaged in classroom interactions. Educators can't wait for the right professional development session to gain needed skills. They need to be proactive in seeking what they don't know with the courage and commitment to try something different.

The internet is available to help educators along with the resources in this guide. With practice, teachers can develop habits to authentically reach and teach all students in a way that shows they genuinely care that all their students will learn. We say that students have no excuses not to learn, but at the same time, teachers (and other adults) now have no excuses not to build competencies and skills they need to learn either!

The structure of schools can be barriers to student learning. This ranges from tracking, many inexperienced teachers, unfair treatment of students, rigid rules applied differently to diverse students, little access to brain-developing skills, etc. Tracking is the practice of grouping students together according to their classroom talents or lacks. Some schools stopped tracking for a while, but as usual, some teachers didn't learn the skills to teach students. Some of them have gone back to ability grouping and tracking since they are familiar with the olden days, but they have to make sure that they don't continue its history of race, class and gender discrimination and privilege that went along with tracking.

A few other influencers/ influences sometimes left unspoken in schools:

1 Some teachers have low expectations of students from diverse groups. They may not believe that all children can learn and may not feel they have the skills to teach them. Of course they don't say this, but students know when teachers and school staff don't like them or feel uncomfortable teaching them. They listen to adult conversations even when adults are not aware and they are familiar with code words used among staff, too. Students can feel what adults (at home, too) think about them so adults need to work to change to their expectations. What you expect, you'll receive!

2 When color blindness is used for supposed racial and income harmony, it ignores children's experiences. When people are invisible,

you will probably overlook them or treat them in a patronizing way, as though they are less than.

3 Bias is a tendency to believe that some people are better than others and it's an unfair personal opinion that influences judgment. Different types of bias are emotional (prejudice); cognitive (stereotypes) and behavioral (discrimination). A few decades ago, bias was more subtle, but now biases are seen more. We're going back in time, nor forward.

Most Americans, including educators, usually hold unexamined biases and prejudices since we assume that it's expected and everybody else like me does it. When prejudiced, we may include people who look like us and exclude others which keeps us from dealing respectfully with diversity. I was told once – "but we don't bring that to school!" Just like parents and other adults, teachers are the same person with the same beliefs and ways of acting at home and at work. Peer pressure and bullying can also be included in adult reactions to diversity.

4 Peer pressure may keep some students from learning if they aren't confident and taught to control their impulses. They need to be aware of possible consequences for their decisions and taught how to resist pressure from others. When teachers allow peer pressure to control classes, they're not using real life as teachable moments. When these issues are dealt with, greater respect for the teacher and other students can sometimes lead to more students willing to learn.

5 Some schools and educators talk about learning, but practice actions that show they don't seem to value learning by all students and use brain research that supports this. This last school influencer can happen at home, too.

Though the above can influence student achievement, along with things you do at home, your children's achievement is not bound by them. It's what else ***you and schools do*** in helping your children develop and learn academically that makes the difference!

There's no reason why children in inner cities or rural areas
do not receive the same quality education or opportunities
as those in suburbs or wealthy neighborhoods.
If we truly believe in giving all citizens
a chance to pursue happiness and pursue their goals,
then we cannot continue to marginalize. –*Al Sharpton*

16. Advocacy Skills and Resources for Every Child to Achieve

When schools don't offer opportunities for students to learn and services are not offered to help students, then students' rights are violated since children have a right to be educated.

This chapter is a step in building advocacy skills so you can speak on behalf of all children by joining together with others. As parents, you have already used individual advocacy skills when talking to teachers on behalf of your child. You probably even had to advocate with family members and friends about making changes in your family as you began to work for more well-being and wellness in your family so your children would have better chances with academic achievement life. So advocacy is not totally new to you in an informal way!

Advocacy is action that speaks in favor or support of, argues for causes, defends or pleads on behalf of others. It is done to make something else happen to bring about desired changes or outcomes. There are three kinds of advocacy. Individual advocacy tries to influence what happens with or for one person through opportunities and services that have to be offered to eligible students. School advocacy is usually about the legal rights of students. Systems advocacy hopes to influence the way things are done for everyone in a school, county, district or state.

When you advocate, you understand that all students need access to good teaching, experiences and resources, especially since each student now has to show academic growth each year. Students who are not achieving academically have unmet needs that have to be met.

We need advocates to help improve our schools, especially since our schools reproduce the inequalities and contradictions in our country. As a result of reading this guide, you know a little more about schooling and how it has changed over time to benefit our nation but not to benefit all the students. You know that public schools were not created for all the students, of the students, and definitely not by all of them. As a parent, you may have some experiences in building skills of advocacy in your quest to make sure that your children are learning.

Advocacy skills follow with underlined words or terms. We now need to shift schooling so it includes your voice as you join with others to form relationships for working together as advocates. You have built confidence in your skills while making decisions that may have differed from your friends and some family members. You stood up for what your family needs. You have learned where and how to find information so you can make more informed decisions for the good of your children and family. You may have moved out of your comfort zone.

You have used effective communication skills while learning to talk with your children about issues of substance and building trust within the family. You have solved problems and taken action. You have analyzed or worked through problems to delegate responsibility. You have used community resources and agencies and you networked with others.

As an advocate, you share experiences, resources and support with other parents and groups and you learn how the system works. You learn public speaking, talking to government officials and presiding over meetings. You plan events and organize other people as you've done in planning actions for successful parenting at home. You apply skills and experiences and advocate in other areas when necessary.

You already have what it takes to begin as a first-class advocate!

Time and scheduling will create new pursuits if you wish, or you may just want to learn more about working more effectively with your children's schools. As you've seen above, you have advocacy skills that can be used to improve schools for everybody's children, not just your own.

Working with others. It's always best when you can advocate with others since it strengthens your cause and you can share resources at times. You can form alliances on common shared interests, or coalitions which are temporary alliances. Collaborations are more 21st century, where you learn and work together with others. No organization is perfect so pay attention to what's being done on behalf of all students, not just some. No matter which type of working together you choose, ask important questions to make sure that your goals are on the same page.

- Does their mission align with your cause and the results you seek?

- Would students and schools be helped by their mission?
- Do they have direct experience or indirect conversations?
- Would it make a difference if this group is involved?
- Will the topic energize more networks or close some of them?

Make tough decisions to work with allies with common interests so relationships can form. Don't get bogged down with many differences.

Community organizing differs from parent involvement or engagement. If you are unsure how to start organizing with others, you can gain those skills. This is the advocacy part of parenting. Read the article, *Transforming Schools through Community Organizing: A Research Review.* [83] In that step by step plan for organizing parents, you'll find information that ranges from selecting a name to what to do if your children experience negative reactions because of your activism.

Grassroots are common or ordinary people who differ from the elite or leadership of already established organizations. If you prefer to work with a grassroots organization, you will first need to find them on-line or ask others in the community. Or you may need to start a grassroots organization with others or strengthen an existing one, if needed. [84]

You may want to recruit teachers and other educators in your school or community who are also advocates for good schools as possibly good allies as mentioned in the ASCD Advocacy Guide (2008). A school organization that seems more in touch with advocacy is the Parent Teacher Association. Its goal is to improve the health, safety, welfare and education of every child. Become an active member of the PTA to influence policy development and to make sure it promotes the interests of all students. If your child's school doesn't have a PTA, the national will help you start one. [85]

Another group that helps parents build advocacy skills is the Mexican American Legal Defense and Educational Fund/NEA (2010). Their toolkit, *Minority Parent & Community Engagement: Best Practices and Policy Recommendations for Closing Gaps in Student Achievement* has topics that may be of interest to you. [86]

Never doubt that a small group of thoughtful committed citizens can change the world: Indeed it's the only thing that ever has.

— Margret Mead

Advocacy Resources. Advocate for the good schools that all children deserve by sharing the following resources that are aligned with school issues. They are for school stakeholders that include your local school board, schools and teachers. Each stakeholder group may find that viewing all the resources gives them a clearer picture since they all have students and their parents in common. Use your computer or one at your local school or public library to find the resources by following directions at Dr. Mapp's website.

I believe that education is the civil rights issue of our generation. And if you care about promoting opportunity and reducing inequality, the classroom is the place to start. Great teaching is about so much more than education; it is a daily fight for social justice. --*Arne Duncan*

School Systems are usually directed by local boards of education under superintendents who may work on behalf of the board. They are supposed to look out for all students and elicit opinions from the community. They should also give information to schools since they are held accountable for school performances. School systems also should be accessible to the public since they spend taxpayer funds to meet students' needs. They need to promote diversity to benefit all students while supporting school staffs.

1. A free guide, *Achieving Educational Excellence for All: A Guide to Diversity-Related Policy Strategies for School Districts* (NSBA, 2011) is available. [87]
2. An infographic series at *Partnerships not Push outs: A Guide for School Board Members* and other resources offers positive alternatives to help improve school systems. [88]
3. View a 12 minute TED [89] (*Changing Education Paradigms*) for one interpretation as to why U.S. schools need to be redesigned.
4. School systems should look outside themselves to learn more about the global achievement gap. [90]
5. Stakeholders should possibly read about sensitive issues at home so they can process what is read in private, [91] with a topic like *Understanding White Privilege* (Kendall, 2001).
6. The title of this article is self-explanatory: *Speak Up At School: How to Respond to Everyday Prejudice, Bias and Stereotypes.* [92]

7. To support parents working in school systems and other businesses, see *Your Workplace: Simple Investment, Big Reward.* Search. [93]

8. *Hard-Won Lessons from* Improving Districts are offered by the Education Trust in a 2014 webinar series.

9. Use the *National Equity Atlas to* learn more about national equity data in large cities and how to use data. [94]

10. Read articles about our commitment to diversity in *Restoring Our Schools* and/or read a review of L. Darling-Hammond's (2010), *The Flat World and Education: How America's Commitment to Equity will Determine Our Future.* [95]

11. Conversations about race are difficult due to societal and internal barriers (Sue, D., 2014, *Race Talk and the Conspiracy of Silence*), but the dialogue is needed. This book may facilitate group dialogue.

A school is a building with four walls, and tomorrow inside.

– Dan Valentine

Schools have to help students prepare for 21st century opportunities and challenges. Needed are engaging academics, critical thinking, an effective management of discipline, positive community awareness of school issues and awareness of student development. They should help students develop civically, emotionally, cognitively, vocationally and socially.

1. Using easier to understand books that don't challenge students nor increase their vocabulary is not differentiating instruction. Teachers in *Core of the Matter: What Does an Equitable Classroom Look Like?* used Common Core State Standards and its emphasis on skills needed after graduation for all students. [96]

2. To ensure that your school is preparing students as needed for life after graduation, see *Prepare High School Students for Successful Transitions to Postsecondary Education and Employment.* [97]

3. Promote positive discipline and healthy relationships in schools through a *Restorative Practices Tool Kit*: Opportunity to Learn 2014. [98]

4. Nine characteristics of schools that are successful in responding to diversity while facilitating learning are in *The Essentials of Diversity Responsive Schools* (Hawley & Wolf, 2011) [99].

5. *Ethnic and Racial Disparities in Education* are reviewed with recommendations. [100]
6. Some schools have gone back to ability grouping and tracking and they need to remember its history to help reduce racial conflicts. [101]
7. Schools undergoing rapid demographic shifts have to build trust; engage in cultural competency; confront social dominance and social justice; transform instructional practices and engage the entire school. (Howard, ASCD. *As Diversity Grows, So Must We*)
8. Teaching and reinforcing responsible human behavior with writing prompts is important for students and their teachers. The books include: Mendler and Curwin. (2004). *Discipline with Dignity*. ASCD and Harmin, M. (2007). *Inspiring Active Learning: A Complete Handbook for Today's Teachers*. ASCD.
9. Tutoring classrooms located in low income communities can help students learn if they are closer to home. (Furchtgott-Roth). [102]
10. *Career technical education provides alternate paths to success* is an important option for some students and important to Common Core. [103]
11. Thinking routines are important at school and need to be integrated with content learning. Use *Project Zero Visible Thinking* with young children (Harvard) to help all children, not just gifted, think. [104]

12. A chart is available to help youth after community violence occurs. [105]

The greatest sign of success for a teacher...
is to be able to say,
'The children are now working as if I did not exist.'
-- Maria Montessori

Teachers in Classrooms: Teachers' self-reflections are important to classroom dynamics and interactions since disconnects exist between classroom practices and students' needs for hands-on learning. This begins with honestly examining personal beliefs and attitudes about working with diverse students, as mentioned in a previous chapter in this part of the book. Both of these inform their core beliefs which can support or keep students from achieving.

Some teachers don't believe they have the skills to teach students from diverse groups. When teachers learn to be unbiased through self-awareness, consciously think about their responses before acting, and once they understand and work for diversity, they can then have more success in teaching all students. This takes will, commitment and courage in our society and schools because of the status quo. Some people already recognize this and have started building the will and courage to do what's necessary. The following documents will be useful to school stakeholders:

1. *Teaching the Teachers: Preparing Educators to Engage Families for Student Achievement* (Harvard Family Research Project, PTA)
2. Check out *Keeping Kids Connected* (2000).
3. Compare curricula and resources to make sure that rigorous instruction is being used in classrooms. Ask five guiding questions: How challenging are the texts used? Do any of them use higher-order thinking? Is PBL or other forms of instruction that require sustained critical thinking being used? What percentage of new materials? What kind of creativity is required? (Blackburn, 2008).
4. Schools with a disproportionate number of students of color need to enlist parents. (Telling Stories, Finding Common Ground). Teachers need to learn how to discipline all students fairly rather than resorting to timeouts where students are sent to other teachers to do so. (*Rethinking Schools*, vol. 29, 1, 2014).
5. *Race and Schools: the Need for Action* is still an issue in today's achievement gaps, no matter where children attend school. [106]
6. Peer-assisted learning strategies make classrooms more responsive to diversity (Fuchs & Fuchs, Mathes, Simmons, 1997).
7. This book is good for introducing sensitive issues to students. *The New Teacher Book: Rethinking Schools.*
8. Course content needs to be rigorous and relevant so that students are prepared for their futures (Jones, *Rigor and Relevance*, 2010).
9. Teachers need to know how to work with parents. This book has strategies for handling five conflicts: Schwartz, N. (2008). *Teacher Chronicles: Confronting the Demands of Students and Parents.*
10. Teacher attitude and performance in the classroom impact the achievement levels of children. See Rodriguez and Bellanca (2006). *What Is It About Me that You Can't Teach? An Instructional Guide for the Urban Educator.* Thousand Oaks, CA: Corwin Press.
11. Children have to believe they can be successful. See the Eight Pathways to Every Child's Success in a useful poster.

The end of this guide book is the beginning of your family's journey to well-being and your children's academic growth for better life chances!

Conclusion

Parents: It's past time to become our BEST selves as we strive to be the BEST teachers of our children. The question is not whether you know what to do to produce positive outcomes with your children. You can find that information anywhere. It's important that you do what's necessary for positive differences in your family for your children's worlds!

Adults and children need a wide range of abilities and behaviors for success today. Hopefully you are now more familiar with the following major clues that were introduced and outlined in this guide for your empowerment as you find the simple within the complexities of our world.

1. ***Continuous learning*** is necessary throughout life to keep up with the new skills that come with change. We need to be creative, innovative and open to change. We need to feel what's happening around us while thinking on different levels to gain solutions to our problems. When working with others, whether in or out of our families, we need to use our clear communication skills so we can understand each other.
2. ***Positive relationships*** are needed since we are not alone as we influence each other and solve problems together, beginning with our families and neighbors, then people from other cultures in our communities, our city, state, nationally and globally. Peace!
3. ***Be positive*** to attract more good things in your life while teaching your children life skills for living and learning. With life skills, children learn to think, adapt, be accountable and learn people skills, social responsibility, ethics and leadership.
4. ***Literacy changes*** as societies change and we have to be flexible enough to accept them. Literacy changes influence our health and environment, global awareness and our finances. We need to become more literate in economics and business; entrepreneurship and citizenship; and information, media, communications and technology to keep up with today's changes.
5. ***Many decisions and choices*** made today are based in our pasts and have consequences for the future. Everything is connected, affecting other things that happen since nothing is isolated. We can't predict and control what's going to happen so we need to be aware of possible consequences for our choices and decisions.

I hope that this guide book has guided you to be the BEST teachers, not just the first teachers, of your children and that it:

- ***Breathed life into you and your family*** as you reflected on your personal and family lives, looked at where you are right now and began, anew, the dreams of where you are going in the future;
- ***Empowered you*** to strengthen your home practices for increased wellness and well-being that focus your feelings and efforts where you want them to be;
- ***Set you on the road*** to raising capable children who are ready to achieve academically so they can overcome any challenges and be ready for opportunities in their futures;
- ***Transformed*** how you see our nation's past and the misconceptions and contradictions that still need to be corrected in our relationships -- and many other areas so we can move beyond where we are to where we need to be!

Our deepest fear is not that we are inadequate.
Our deepest fear is that we are powerful beyond measure.
It is our light, not our darkness that most frightens us.
We ask ourselves,
Who am I to be brilliant, gorgeous, talented, fabulous?
Actually, who are you not *to be?* *–Marianne Williamson*
(Quoted by President Nelson Mandela in his inauguration speech)

Did you possess the courage, the will and the commitment to do what's needed for the good of your children with this guidebook? Yes or No – if yes, congrats, if no, when will you?

It all begins with YOU as Your Child's BEST Teacher!

Discussion Guide

1. Did you notice anything surprising with Part I's interpretation of history? How does it fit with what you've been taught? Did it answer any questions you've had? Was it realistic or not?
2. Ask your family – how does your family history fit with this one?
3. Which misconceptions and contradictions in your family may need to change? Or do you think the history you learned is more accurate? How about the relationship part? How is that important, or not, to you?
4. Take time to really think and feel your responses to *Getting Started.* Where are you as parents in this list? Ask your family about it.
5. Was the holistic approach too much? Or is it complex like life? How?
6. Why is it important to take time now to look at how we parent, rear or raise our children? Have you made promises before but didn't do it?
7. What kind of impact do you want education to have on your children? Are you working to make it come true? Was this book helpful?
8. Re-read the *Parts* as introductions to the chapters. Ask your family how they feel about the topics. Do they guide you to improve?
9. Was the chapter on proficiency easy to understand? How does it fit with your life? Does it help you help your children more? Confusing?
10. Notice that some things are repeated in *Home Preparations*? Which areas are most important to you right now? How about your children?
11. Do you serve as an advocate for other children or "give back?"
12. Do you consciously think about what you're going to do, or do you go with the flow most of the time? Do you want your children to do that?
13. Are you keeping a journal and writing in the book? Are you serious?
14. Were the adult choices useful to you? Did you develop your own action plan and time line, and do it! You can change your future if you choose to!
15. Have you prepared yourself for hard questions or topics you may be uncomfortable with that were brought up in the book? How? When? Have you taken the time to talk and future-plan with them? Practice what to say here, write it down- do it!
16. Do you need to go back to school?
17. Was this book helpful to you or not? Send comments. [107]
18. Have you started writing your family's story yet?

Selected References

Barksdale, I. D. (2014). *Close Your Eyes*. True Perspectives.

Boggs, G.L. and J. (2014). *Revolution and Evolution in the 21st Century.*

Burant, T., Christensen, L., Salas. K. D., & Walters S. (2010). *The New Teacher Book: Finding Purpose, Balance, and Hope During Your First Years in the Classroom*. Rethinking Schools.

Embry, I. A. (2014). *Balancing the Rift: Reconnectualizing the Pasenture.*

Embry, O. N. (2013). *Expanding Horizons Through Creative Expressions.*

GRAND Magazine: The Magazine for Grandparents, free online.

Hamlyn. (2009). *The Best Ever Games for Kids: 501 Ways to Have Fun.*

Kurashige, S. & Boggs, G. L. (2012). *The Next American Revolution: Sustainable Activism for the Twenty-First Century.* U of California.

Mapp, J.R. (In Press). *Chance or Circumstance: The Memoirs of A Civil Rights Activist.* (My Daddy's book!)

McClain, V. P. (2009/2013). *The Intentional Parenting Plan* and *Your Presence is Requested: Critical Essays on Parenting and Education.*

Menkart, D., Murray, A.D., and View, J. L., Eds. (2004). *Putting the Movement Back into Civil Rights Teaching: A Resource Guide*

National Governors Association Center for Best Practices, CCSSO. (2010). *Common Core State Standards*. Washington DC.

Noguera, P. (2003). *City Schools and the American Dream: Reclaiming the Promise of Public Education.* New York: TCP.

Pugach, M. C. (2006). *Because Teaching Matters*. John Wiley & Sons.

Quisenberry, R.L. (2002). *ASagaoftheBlackMan.com plus others*

Rethinking Schools. Many books on needed topics. rethinkingschools.com

Schwarz, E. (2014).*The Opportunity Equation: How Citizen Teachers Are Combating the Achievement Gap in America's Schools*. Beacon.

Search Institute. (2006). *40 Developmental Assets*. For ages 3 - 18.

Snyder, K.J., Acker-Hocevarl, M., and Snyder, K.R. (2000). *Living on the Edge of Chaos: Leading Schools into the Global Age.* ASQ Quality.

Takaki, R. (1993). *A Different Mirror: A History of Multicultural America.* Read Chapter 1. [108]

Tsabary, S. (2010).*The Conscious Parent*. Transforming parents.

Virginia Commonwealth University. (2000). *Going to College: A Resource for Teens with Disabilities.* Code: Gratitude

Certificate of Book Completion

CERTIFICATE OF BOOK COMPLETION

The parents of the

____

Family
do hereby certify that
we are ready and willing with
to begin or continue our journey as the

BEST Teachers

for our children, who will work to be the

BEST Children

in our Family!

Signed with by Family Members

____

____

____

____

____

OUR BEST FUTURE IS COMING....

See [109] for a nicer certificate!

I'm proud of you for taking steps to move your family into this new time in history, knowing that you will take actions to become even more successful in your most important job! -- ***Dr. Mapp***

Final Notes

See Dr. Mapp's author website for links that give more information about topics that were introduced in this short guidebook. I'm impressed with the websites [X] and know they'll help you to guide your family to the next level. If they don't help you, know that there are plenty of sites that will give you what you need so just search for them online or in books at the local library. You may find you need to reach out to helping professionals when your family has certain problems like mental issues, or you see that problems are deeper than the surface!

I know that there are a lot of sites, but select the ones that are most useful to your family. Some of them may teach you new skills, and some of them may be reminders to help you tweak the good things you do as you parent.

It's all good!

Continue with lifelong learning
to improve your family's well-being, wellness
and ultimately your lifestyle,
if it's not where you dream your family to be!

Remember…
When you love yourself enough to make positive differences
with your family, loved ones and other relationships,
it will all be good!
Sure there'll still be crises and bad days,
but you know that you have what it takes to help your family
bounce back into the good things!

Academic achievement and more chances for your children
to have good lives in their futures is all worth it!

Peace, love, blessings, gratitude, prosperity,
hope and giving to all of you!
---Dr. DeBora L'Tanya Mapp